Taste of Home

EVERYDAY CHICKEN

EDITORIAL
EDITOR-IN-CHIEF: Catherine Cassidy
CREATIVE DIRECTOR: Howard Greenberg
EDITORIAL OPERATIONS DIRECTOR: Kerri Balliet

MANAGING EDITOR/PRINT AND DIGITAL BOOKS: Mark Hagen
ASSOCIATE CREATIVE DIRECTOR: Edwin Robles Jr.

EDITOR: Heather Ray
ASSOCIATE EDITOR: Christine Rukavena
CONTRIBUTING ART DIRECTOR: Siya Motamedi
EDITORIAL PRODUCTION MANAGER: Dena Ahlers
COPY CHIEF: Deb Warlaumont Mulvey
CONTRIBUTING COPY EDITOR: Mary-Liz Shaw

CHIEF FOOD EDITOR: Karen Berner
FOOD EDITORS: James Schend; Peggy Woodward, RD
ASSOCIATE FOOD EDITOR: Krista Lanphier
RECIPE EDITORS: Mary King; Annie Rundle; Jenni Sharp, RD; Irene Yeh
CONTENT OPERATIONS MANAGER: Colleen King
CONTENT OPERATIONS ASSISTANT: Shannon Stroud
EXECUTIVE ASSISTANT: Marie Brannon

TEST KITCHEN AND FOOD STYLING MANAGER: Sarah Thompson
TEST COOKS: Nicholas Iverson (lead), Matthew Hass, Lauren Knoelke
FOOD STYLISTS: Kathryn Conrad (senior), Shannon Roum, Leah Rekau
PREP COOKS: Megumi Garcia, Melissa Hansen, Nicole Spohrleder, Bethany Jacobson

PHOTOGRAPHY DIRECTOR: Stephanie Marchese
PHOTOGRAPHERS: Dan Roberts, Jim Wieland
PHOTOGRAPHER/SET STYLIST: Grace Natoli Sheldon
SET STYLISTS: Stacey Genaw, Melissa Haberman, Dee Dee Jacq

BUSINESS ANALYST: Kristy Martin
BILLING SPECIALIST: Mary Ann Koebernik

BUSINESS
GENERAL MANAGER, TASTE OF HOME COOKING SCHOOLS: Erin Puariea
VICE PRESIDENT, BRAND MARKETING: Jennifer Smith
VICE PRESIDENT, CIRCULATION AND CONTINUITY MARKETING: Dave Fiegel

READER'S DIGEST NORTH AMERICA
VICE PRESIDENT, BUSINESS DEVELOPMENT AND MARKETING: Alain Begun
PRESIDENT, BOOKS AND HOME ENTERTAINMENT: Harold Clarke
GENERAL MANAGER, CANADA: Philippe Cloutier
VICE PRESIDENT, OPERATIONS: Mitch Cooper
CHIEF OPERATING OFFICER: Howard Halligan
VICE PRESIDENT, CHIEF SALES OFFICER: Mark Josephson
VICE PRESIDENT, GENERAL MANAGER, MILWAUKEE: Frank Quigley
VICE PRESIDENT, DIGITAL SALES: Steve Sottile
VICE PRESIDENT, CHIEF CONTENT OFFICER: Liz Vaccariello
VICE PRESIDENT, GLOBAL FINANCIAL PLANNING AND ANALYSIS: Devin White

THE READER'S DIGEST ASSOCIATION, INC.
PRESIDENT AND CHIEF EXECUTIVE OFFICER: Robert E. Guth

© 2014 REIMAN MEDIA GROUP, INC.
5400 S. 60TH ST., GREENDALE WI 53129

INTERNATIONAL STANDARD BOOK NUMBER:
978-1-61765-268-4
LIBRARY OF CONGRESS CONTROL NUMBER: 2013910106
COMPONENT NUMBER: 116000210H00

PRINTED IN U.S.A.
1 3 5 7 9 10 8 6 4 2

PICTURED ON THE FRONT COVER:
Roast Chicken Breasts with Peppers, page 73; Spring-Thyme Chicken Stew, page 94; Honey-Mustard Chicken Sandwiches, page 29
PICTURED ON THE BACK COVER:
Thai Chicken Lettuce Wraps, page 100; Slow-Cooked Chicken Chili, page 91; Thai Chicken Pizza, page 68

Chicken Saves the Day

It's the one thing my family can agree on. Whether it's in a soothing soup on a chilly day or a comforting homemade potpie, chicken has earned its title as our dinnertime hero.

Now, with more than 175 chicken recipes and tips in *Taste of Home Everyday Chicken,* you, too, can take advantage of this versatile mainstay and enjoy new family-pleasing dishes for any occasion. Think casseroles, stews, slow-cooked suppers and saucy oven entrees. Whether you're feeding a crowd or cooking for one or two (look for the Serves 1 or 2 icon throughout this book), you'll never be short of great-tasting options.

Because the dishes in this book come from home cooks across the country, you can count on family-friendly flavors and practical cooking methods. And each recipe comes with the Taste of Home Test Kitchen-guarantee. (Yes, that means we've tested and tasted each one!)

Looking for a quick dinner tonight? Try the Chicken Provolone (p. 73) sent to us from Dawn Bryant in Thedford, Nebraska. Ready in just 25 minutes, it's one of her husband's best-loved suppers. Or, next time you have leftover chicken, whip up Rickey Madden's Baked Chicken Chimichangas (p. 60). If that recipe doesn't become your new favorite dinner, we're sure you'll find one that will.

Enjoy!

Catherine

P.S. Do you have a family recipe you'd like to share with Taste of Home? Stop by tasteofhome.com/submit to introduce yourself and upload your recipe.

THAI CHICKEN LETTUCE WRAPS PAGE 100

CHICKEN POTPIE PAGE 63

CHICKEN ENCHILADA SOUP PAGE 16

MAPLE-GLAZED WINGS PAGE 12

CHICKEN & MUSHROOM CREPES PAGE 100

f **LIKE US** facebook.com/tasteofhome

VISIT OUR BLOG loveandhomemaderecipes.com

TWEET US @tasteofhome

SHOP WITH US shoptasteofhome.com

P **FOLLOW US** pinterest.com/taste_of_home

SHARE A RECIPE tasteofhome.com/submit

Table of Contents

CHICKEN FLORENTINE MEATBALLS
PAGE 79

**MAPLE-GLAZED
WINGS**
PAGE 12

Appetizers & Munchies

ASIAN CHICKEN
DUMPLINGS

Chicken Club Ring

I found this recipe years ago and recently started making it lighter by using fat-free mayonnaise and reduced-fat cheese. We think it's just as tasty.

—REBECCA CLARK WARRIOR, AL

PREP: 20 MIN. • **BAKE:** 20 MIN.
MAKES: 16 SERVINGS

- ½ cup mayonnaise
- 1 Tbsp. minced fresh parsley
- 2 tsp. Dijon mustard
- 1½ tsp. finely chopped onion
- 1¾ cups cubed cooked chicken breast (½-in. cubes)
- 2 bacon strips, cooked and crumbled
- 1 cup (4 oz.) shredded Swiss cheese, divided
- 2 tubes (8 oz. each) refrigerated crescent roll
- 2 plum tomatoes
- 2 cups shredded lettuce

1. In a large bowl, combine the mayonnaise, parsley, mustard and onion. Stir in the chicken, bacon and ¾ cup cheese.

2. Unroll crescent dough; separate into 16 triangles. Arrange on ungreased 12-in. round pizza pan, forming a ring with pointed ends facing outer edge of pan and wide ends overlapping.

3. Spoon chicken mixture over wide ends; fold points over filling and tuck under wide ends (filling will be visible). Chop half of a tomato; set aside. Slice remaining tomatoes; place over filling and tuck into dough.

4. Bake at 375° for 20-25 minutes or until golden brown. Sprinkle with remaining cheese. Let stand for 5 minutes. Place lettuce in center of ring; sprinkle with chopped tomato.

Asian Chicken Dumpling

To celebrate my two daughters' Chinese heritage, we occasionally make Chinese food, especially around holidays like Chinese New Year. I took a traditional pork dumpling recipe and modified it using ground chicken.

—JOY OLCOTT MILLERSVILLE, PA

PREP: 40 MIN. • **COOK:** 10 MIN./BATCH
MAKES: 2½ DOZEN

- 1 lb. ground chicken
- 4 green onions, chopped
- ½ cup chopped cabbage
- ¼ cup minced fresh cilantro
- 2 tsp. minced fresh gingerroot
- 1 tsp. salt
- ¼ tsp. Chinese five-spice powder
- 2 Tbsp. water

- 1 pkg. (10 oz.) pot sticker or gyoza wrappers
  Cabbage leaves
  Reduced-sodium soy sauce

1. Place the first seven ingredients in a food processor; cover and process until finely chopped. Add water; cover and process until blended.

2. Place 1 Tbsp. chicken mixture in the center of one wrapper. (Keep remaining wrappers covered with a damp paper towel to prevent them from drying out.) Moisten edges with water. Fold wrapper over filling to form a semicircle; press edges firmly to seal, pleating the front side to form three to five folds.

3. Holding sealed edges, stand each dumpling on an even surface; press to flatten bottom. Repeat with remaining wrappers and filling; cover dumplings with plastic wrap.

4. Line a steamer basket with four cabbage leaves. Arrange dumplings in batches 1 in. apart over cabbage; place in a large saucepan over 1 in. of water. Bring to a boil; cover and steam for 10-12 minutes or until a thermometer reads 165°. Discard cabbage. Repeat. Serve with soy sauce.

CHICKEN CLUB RING

Mexican Chicken Meatballs

These low-fat meatballs taste fabulous on their own, but if you want to take things up a notch, serve them with a dip of hot Velveeta cheese and salsa.

—**KATRINA LOPES** LYMAN, SC

PREP: 20 MIN. • **BAKE:** 15 MIN.
MAKES: ABOUT 5 DOZEN

- ½ cup egg substitute
- 1 can (4 ounces) chopped green chilies
- 1 cup crushed cornflakes
- 1 cup (4 ounces) shredded reduced-fat Mexican cheese blend
- ½ teaspoon seasoned salt
- ¼ teaspoon cayenne pepper
- 1 pound ground chicken
  Salsa, optional

1. In a large bowl, combine the first six ingredients. Crumble chicken over mixture and mix well. Shape into 1-in. balls. Place on baking sheets coated with cooking spray.

2. Bake at 375° for 12-15 minutes or until a meat thermometer reads 165° and juices run clear, turning occasionally. Serve with salsa if desired.

FREEZE OPTION *Freeze cooled meatballs in freezer containers. To use, partially thaw in refrigerator overnight. Microwave, covered, on high in a microwave-safe dish until heated through, gently stirring and adding a little broth or water if necessary.*

 Did you know?
With around 20 billion chickens in the world, there are almost three times more chickens than humans on the planet.

Chicken Skewers with Cool Avocado Sauce

I'm always looking for lighter recipes to take on tailgate outings. And this one works great for grilling. Just whip up the marinade, add the chicken and take it along to the pregame festivities.

—**VERONICA CALLAGHAN** GLASTONBURY, CT

PREP: 25 MIN. + MARINATING
GRILL: 10 MIN.
MAKES: 16 SKEWERS (¾ CUP SAUCE)

- 1 pound boneless skinless chicken breasts
- ½ cup lime juice
- 1 tablespoon balsamic vinegar
- 2 teaspoons minced chipotle pepper in adobo sauce
- ½ teaspoon salt

SAUCE
- 1 medium ripe avocado, peeled and pitted
- ½ cup fat-free sour cream
- 2 tablespoons minced fresh cilantro
- 2 teaspoons lime juice
- 1 teaspoon grated lime peel
- ¼ teaspoon salt

1. Flatten chicken to ¼-in. thickness; cut lengthwise into sixteen 1-in.-wide strips. In a large resealable plastic bag, combine the lime juice, vinegar, chipotle pepper and salt; add the chicken. Seal bag and turn to coat; refrigerate for 30 minutes.

2. Meanwhile, for the sauce, place remaining ingredients in a food processor; cover and process until blended. Transfer to a serving bowl; cover and refrigerate until serving.

3. Drain and discard marinade from chicken. Thread meat onto four metal or soaked wooden skewers. Moisten a paper towel with cooking oil; using long-handled tongs, lightly coat the grill rack. Grill, covered, over medium heat or broil 4 in. from the heat for 8-12 minutes or until no longer pink, turning frequently. Serve with sauce.

CHICKEN SKEWERS WITH COOL AVOCADO SAUCE

Sesame Nuggets with Honey Mayo

Between working and raising three children, we don't have much time on our hands. These crunchy chicken bites can be prepared in a hurry for a super snack or light dinner.

—**DONNA SHULL** PIPERSVILLE, PA

START TO FINISH: 30 MIN. • **MAKES:** 6-8 SERVING

- ½ cup fine dry bread crumb
- ¼ cup sesame seed
- ½ cup mayonnaise
- 1 tsp. dried minced onion
- 1 tsp. ground mustard
- 4 cups cubed cooked chicken breast

SAUCE
- ½ cup mayonnaise
- ¼ cup honey

1. In a large resealable plastic bag, combine bread crumbs and sesame seeds; set aside. In a small bowl, combine the mayonnaise, onion and mustard. Coat chicken pieces with mayonnaise mixture, then toss in crumb mixture.

2. Place on a greased baking sheet. Bake at 425° for 10-12 minutes or until lightly browned. Combine sauce ingredients; serve with chicken.

SESAME NUGGETS WITH HONEY MAYO

For Super Bowl parties, this is my go-to dip. My family loves it, and everywhere I take it people ask for the recipe.

—**PEGGY FOSTER** FLORENCE, KY

BUFFALO CHICKEN DIP

Buffalo Chicken Dip

START TO FINISH: 30 MIN. • **MAKES:** ABOUT 2 CUPS

- 1 package (8 ounces) cream cheese, softened
- 1 can (10 ounces) chunk white chicken, drained
- ½ cup buffalo wing sauce
- ½ cup ranch salad dressing
- 2 cups (8 ounces) shredded Colby-Monterey Jack cheese
  French bread baguette slices, celery ribs or tortilla chips, optional

1. Preheat oven to 350°. Spread cream cheese into an ungreased shallow 1-qt. baking dish. Layer with chicken, wing sauce and salad dressing. Sprinkle with cheese.

2. Bake, uncovered, 20-25 minutes or until cheese is melted. If desired, serve with baguette slices.

Chicken, Pear & Gorgonzola Tarts

I was experimenting with candied bacon and tried incorporating it into some of my favorite recipes. These little bites were created during the holiday season and were quickly gobbled up.

—**KATHLEEN BOULANGER** WILLISTON, VERMONT

PREP: 30 MIN. • **COOK:** 5 MIN. • **MAKES:** 2½ DOZEN

- 8 bacon strip
- 1½ tsp. brown sugar
- ¼ tsp. ground cinnamon
- ¾ cup finely chopped cooked chicken breast
- ⅓ cup pear nectar
- ¼ cup finely chopped dried pear
- 3 Tbsp. apricot preserve
- 2 tsp. butter
- ¼ tsp. salt
- ¼ tsp. pepper
- 2 pkg. (1.9 oz. each) frozen miniature phyllo tart shell
- ⅓ cup crumbled Gorgonzola cheese

1. Place bacon in a 15-in. x 10-in. x 1-in. baking pan; broil 4 in. from the heat for 4-6 minutes on each side or until crisp. Combine brown sugar and cinnamon; sprinkle over bacon. Broil 1 minute longer or until bacon is glazed and bubbly. Drain on paper towels. Cool slightly and crumble.

2. In a small skillet, combine the chicken, pear nectar, pears, preserves, butter, salt and pepper. Bring to a boil; cook, stirring occasionally, for 3-4 minutes or until thickened. Spoon about 1 teaspoonful of filling into each tart shell; place tarts on a baking sheet. Sprinkle with bacon and cheese.

3. Bake at 350° for 5-7 minutes or until heated through. Serve warm.

CHICKEN, PEAR &
GORGONZOLA TART

Bacon-Chicken Club Pizza

Drizzled in a creamy ranch dressing, this pizza has everything you love about a club sandwich in appetizer form. It's a favorite for using up rotisserie chicken.

—**DEBBIE REID** CLEARWATER, FL

START TO FINISH: 25 MIN. • **MAKES:** 8 SLICES

- 1 prebaked 12-inch pizza crust
- 4 ounces cream cheese, softened
- 1 shallot, minced
- 2 cups shredded rotisserie chicken
- 1½ cups (6 ounces) shredded Monterey Jack cheese
- 1 cup (4 ounces) shredded sharp cheddar cheese
- 8 slices ready-to-serve fully cooked bacon, cut into 1-inch pieces
- ¼ cup sour cream
- 3 tablespoons 2% milk
- 2 teaspoons ranch salad dressing mix
- 1 cup shredded lettuce
- 1 plum tomato, seeded and chopped

1. Place crust on an ungreased pizza pan. Combine cream cheese and shallot; spread over crust. Top with chicken, cheeses and bacon.

2. Bake at 425° for 12-15 minutes or until edges are lightly browned and cheese is melted.

3. Meanwhile, in a small bowl, combine the sour cream, milk and dressing mix. Sprinkle lettuce and tomato over pizza; drizzle with dressing.

MAPLE-GLAZED WINGS

Delightful Chicken Salad

You can serve this chicken salad on bread, buns or wrapped in a tortilla. My husband likes it on crackers as a snack or on a bed of lettuce.

—JACKLYN SALGADO OMAHA, NE

PREP: 30 MIN. + CHILLING
MAKES: 2 SERVINGS

- 1 **boneless skinless chicken breast half (6 ounces)**
- ½ **medium onion, chopped**
- 1 **celery rib, chopped**
- 2 **teaspoons chicken bouillon granules**
- 1 **garlic clove, minced**
  Dash pepper

DRESSING
- ½ **cup mayonnaise**
- 1 **to 2 tablespoons minced fresh cilantro**
- 2 **tablespoons finely chopped onion**
  Dash salt and pepper
  Assorted crackers, optional

1. In a large saucepan, combine the chicken, onion, celery, bouillon, garlic and pepper; add water to cover by 1 in. Bring to a boil. Reduce heat; cover and simmer for 15-20 minutes or until a meat thermometer reads 170°. Drain, reserving the onion, celery and garlic. Shred chicken and place in a bowl; add reserved onion mixture.

2. In a small bowl, combine the mayonnaise, cilantro, onion, salt and pepper. Spoon over chicken mixture; gently stir to coat. Cover and refrigerate until chilled. Serve with crackers if desired.

Or Bake the Wings

If the weather's not on your side or you don't have a grill, you can bake the Maple-Glazed Wings in the oven at 375° for 30-40 minutes or until juices run clear.

Maple-Glazed Wings

Some wonderful maple syrup I brought back from a trip to Vermont is what inspired this recipe. I serve them as TV snacks, hors d'oeuvres for showers and backyard party appetizers.

—JANICE HENCK CLARKSTON, GA

PREP: 10 MIN. + MARINATING
GRILL: 20 MIN. • **MAKES:** 6-8 SERVINGS

- 2 **to 3 pounds whole chicken wings**
- 1 **cup maple syrup**
- ⅔ **cup chili sauce**
- ½ **cup finely chopped onion**
- 2 **tablespoons Dijon mustard**
- 2 **teaspoons Worcestershire sauce**
- ¼ **to ½ teaspoon crushed red pepper flakes**

1. Cut chicken wings into three sections; discard wing tip section. In a large resealable plastic bag, combine remaining ingredients. Set aside 1 cup for basting and refrigerate. Add chicken to remaining marinade. Seal bag and turn to coat; refrigerate for 4 hours, turning occasionally.

2. Drain and discard marinade. Moisten a paper towel with cooking oil; using long-handled tongs, lightly coat the grill rack. Grill chicken, covered, over medium heat or broil 4 in. from the heat for 12-16 minutes, turning occasionally. Brush with reserved marinade. Grill or broil, uncovered, for 8-10 minutes or until juices run clear, basting and turning several times.

Grilled Tandoori Chicken Kabobs

When I prepare this recipe for Tandoori Chicken it brings back memories of my childhood and my rich Indian heritage. This has a nice spice level, but if you like your food on the mild side, then reduce each spice a little.

—RAVINDER AUJLA GRIDLEY, CA

PREP: 30 MIN. + MARINATING
GRILL: 10 MIN. • **MAKES:** 6 SERVINGS

- 1¼ cups plain yogurt
- ⅓ cup chopped onion
- 2 tablespoons lemon juice
- 2 garlic cloves, minced
- 2 teaspoons garam masala
- 2 teaspoons minced fresh gingerroot
- 1 teaspoon salt
- 1 teaspoon cayenne pepper
- 3 drops yellow food coloring, optional
- 3 drops red food coloring, optional
- 2 pounds boneless skinless chicken breasts, cut into 1-inch cubes
- 2 teaspoons minced fresh cilantro
- 1 medium lemon, cut into six wedges

1. In a large resealable plastic bag, combine the first 10 ingredients. Add the chicken; seal bag and turn to coat. Refrigerate for at least 8 hours or overnight.
2. Drain and discard marinade. Thread chicken onto six metal or soaked wooden skewers. Moisten a paper towel with cooking oil; using long-handled tongs, lightly coat the grill rack.
3. Grill chicken, covered, over medium heat or broil 4 in. from the heat for 10-15 minutes or until juices run clear, turning occasionally. Sprinkle with cilantro; garnish with lemon wedges.
NOTE *Look for garam masala in the spice aisle.*

Make-Ahead Wontons

I sometimes turn this appetizer into a main course by using egg roll wrappers and serving the rolls with a side of chicken gravy.

—MARY KAY DIXSON DECATUR, AL

PREP: 40 MIN. + FREEZING • **BAKE:** 15 MIN.
MAKES: ABOUT 4 DOZEN

- 1 package (3 ounces) cream cheese, softened
- 6 tablespoons butter, softened, divided
- 2 tablespoons minced chives
- ½ teaspoon lemon-pepper seasoning
- 1½ cups finely chopped cooked chicken
- 1 can (4 ounces) mushroom stems and pieces, drained and chopped
- 1 package (12 ounces) wonton wrappers
- ⅔ cup crushed salad croutons
  Sweet-and-sour sauce, optional

1. In a small bowl, beat the cream cheese, 2 tablespoons butter, chives and lemon-pepper until blended. Stir in chicken and mushrooms.
2. Place a rounded teaspoonful in the center of a wonton wrapper. (Keep remaining wrappers covered with a damp paper towel until ready to use.) Fold bottom corner over filling; fold sides toward center. Moisten remaining corner with water; roll up tightly to seal.
3. Melt remaining butter; brush over wontons. Coat with croutons. Place on a baking sheet; freeze. Transfer to a large freezer bag; seal and freeze for up to 3 months.

TO USE FROZEN WONTONS *Place wontons on greased baking sheets. Bake at 425° for 10 minutes. Turn; bake 5-10 minutes longer or until lightly browned. Serve warm with sweet-and-sour sauce if desired.*

MAKE-AHEAD WONTONS

**MEXICAN CHICKEN SOUP
WITH CILANTRO DUMPLINGS**
PAGE 21

Soups, Stews & Chilis

CHICKEN ENCHILADA SOUP

West African Chicken Stew

I really love African flavors, but you don't really encounter them much in America. Here the combination of native African ingredients, all of which are readily accessible to Americans, transports you to a new culinary place.
—**MICHAEL COHEN** LOS ANGELES, CA

PREP: 20 MIN. • **COOK:** 30 MIN.
MAKES: 8 SERVINGS (2½ QUARTS)

- 1 pound boneless skinless chicken breasts, cut into 1-inch cubes
- ½ teaspoon salt
- ¼ teaspoon pepper
- 3 teaspoons canola oil, divided
- 1 medium onion, thinly sliced
- 6 garlic cloves, minced
- 2 tablespoons minced fresh gingerroot
- 2 cans (15½ ounces each) black-eyed peas, rinsed and drained
- 1 can (28 ounces) crushed tomatoes
- 1 large sweet potato, peeled and cut into 1-inch cubes
- 1 cup reduced-sodium chicken broth
- ¼ cup creamy peanut butter
- 1½ teaspoons minced fresh thyme, divided, or ½ teaspoon dried thyme
- ¼ teaspoon cayenne pepper
  Hot cooked brown rice, optional

1. Sprinkle chicken with salt and pepper. In a Dutch oven, cook chicken over medium heat in 2 teaspoons oil for 4-6 minutes or until no longer pink; remove and set aside.
2. In the same pan, saute onion in remaining oil until tender. Add garlic and ginger; cook 1 minute longer.
3. Stir in peas, tomatoes, sweet potato, broth, peanut butter, 1¼ teaspoons fresh thyme (or ½ teaspoon dried thyme) and cayenne. Bring to a boil. Reduce heat; cover and simmer for 15-20 minutes or until potato is tender. Add chicken; heat through.
4. Serve with rice if desired. Sprinkle with remaining fresh thyme.

Chicken Enchilada Soup

Whenever I go to Chili's, I always order the Chicken Enchilada Soup, so I decided to try my hand at a healthier version at home.
—**TRACI CAMPBELL** SAGINAW, TX

PREP: 30 MIN. • **COOK:** 25 MIN.
MAKES: 6 SERVINGS

TOPPING
- 2 corn tortillas (6 inches)
- ½ teaspoon canola oil
- ½ teaspoon chili powder
- ⅛ teaspoon salt
- ⅛ teaspoon cayenne pepper

SOUP
- 1 medium onion, chopped
- 1 tablespoon canola oil
- 1 garlic clove, minced
- 5 cups water, divided
- 2 teaspoons reduced-sodium chicken base
- 1 teaspoon chili powder
- ½ teaspoon ground cumin
- ¼ teaspoon ground coriander
- ⅛ teaspoon cayenne pepper
- ⅓ cup masa harina
- 8 ounces reduced-fat process cheese (Velveeta), cubed
- 2 cups cubed cooked chicken breast
- ¾ cup pico de gallo
- 6 tablespoons shredded Colby-Monterey Jack cheese

1. Cut each tortilla lengthwise into thirds; cut each widthwise into ¼-in. strips. Place strips and oil in a resealable plastic bag; shake to coat. Combine chili powder, salt and cayenne. Add to bag; shake to coat.
2. Arrange tortilla strips on a baking sheet coated with cooking spray. Bake at 400° for 6-8 minutes or until crisp, stirring once. Remove to paper towels to cool; set aside.
3. Meanwhile, in a Dutch oven, saute onion in oil until tender. Add garlic; cook 1 minute longer. Stir in 4 cups water, chicken base, chili powder, cumin, coriander and cayenne. Whisk masa harina and remaining water until smooth; stir into pan. Bring to a boil; cook and stir for 2 minutes or until slightly thickened.
4. Reduce heat. Stir in process cheese until melted. Add chicken; heat through. Ladle into bowls. Top with pico de gallo, shredded cheese and tortilla strips.

WEST AFRICAN CHICKEN STEW

Easy Egg Drop Soup

Who wants takeout when it tastes better homemade? This quick and easy soup is ideal for chilly days. You'll love the addition of tender chicken.

—TASTE OF HOME TEST KITCHEN

PREP: 10 MIN. • **COOK:** 30 MIN.
MAKES: 1 SERVING.

- 1½ cups reduced-sodium chicken broth
- 1 slice peeled fresh gingerroot (¼ inch thick)
- 1 small garlic clove, peeled
- 1½ teaspoons cornstarch
- 1 tablespoon water
- ¼ cup cubed cooked chicken
- 1 egg, lightly beaten
- 1 tablespoon sliced green onion

1. In a small saucepan, combine the broth, ginger and garlic; bring to a boil. Reduce heat; simmer, uncovered, for 15 minutes. Remove and discard ginger and garlic.
2. Combine cornstarch and water until smooth; gradually stir into broth. Bring to a boil; cook and stir for 2 minutes or until thickened. Add chicken; heat through. Reduce heat. Drizzle beaten egg into hot broth, stirring constantly. Remove from the heat; stir in onion.

Chicken and Andouille Gumbo

PREP: 40 MIN. • **COOK:** 2 HOURS
MAKES: 9 SERVINGS (3¼ QUARTS)

- 2 tablespoons Cajun seasoning, divided
- 1 teaspoon salt, divided
- ½ teaspoon pepper, divided
- 3 pounds bone-in chicken thighs, skin removed
- ½ cup plus 2 tablespoons canola oil, divided
- ½ cup all-purpose flour
- 1 large onion, finely chopped
- ¾ cup finely chopped green pepper
- ¾ cup finely chopped sweet red pepper
- 2 celery ribs, finely chopped
- 4 garlic cloves, minced
- 4 cups water

- 2 cups chicken stock
- 1½ pounds fully cooked andouille sausage links, sliced
- 2 tablespoons Worcestershire sauce
- 2 bay leaves
  Hot cooked rice
- 3 green onions, chopped

1. In a small bowl, mix 1 tablespoon Cajun seasoning, ½ teaspoon salt and ¼ teaspoon pepper; rub over chicken. In a Dutch oven, brown chicken in 2 tablespoons oil in batches; remove chicken from pan.
2. Add remaining oil to the same pan; stir in flour until blended. Cook and stir over medium-low heat for 30 minutes or until browned (do not burn). Add onion, peppers and celery; cook and stir for 2-3 minutes or until vegetables are tender. Add garlic; cook 1 minute longer.
3. Gradually add water and stock. Stir in the sausage, Worcestershire sauce, bay leaves, chicken and the remaining Cajun seasoning, salt and pepper. Bring to a boil. Reduce heat; cover and simmer for 1 hour or until chicken is very tender.
4. Remove chicken from pan; cool slightly. Skim fat from soup and discard bay leaves. Shred chicken and return to soup; heat through. Discard bones. Serve gumbo over rice; top with green onions.

This is my wife's favorite! We pair it with corn bread or a crusty French bread. Who could ask for any more than that?

—**BILLY HENSLEY** MOUNT CARMEL, TN

CHICKEN AND ANDOUILLE GUMBO

Brunswick Stew

This thick stew is filled to the brim with a bounty of potatoes, lima beans, corn and tomatoes. Authentic versions call for rabbit or squirrel, but I think you'll enjoy my recipe calling for tender chunks of chicken.

—MILDRED SHERRER FORT WORTH, TX

PREP: 1 HOUR + COOLING • **COOK:** 45 MIN. • **MAKES:** 6 SERVINGS

- 1 broiler/fryer chicken (3½ to 4 pounds), cut up
- 2 cups water
- 4 medium potatoes, peeled and cubed
- 2 medium onions, sliced
- 1 can (15¼ ounces) lima beans, rinsed and drained
- 1 teaspoon salt
- ½ teaspoon pepper
  Dash cayenne pepper
- 1 can (15¼ ounces) corn, drained
- 1 can (14½ ounces) diced tomatoes, undrained
- ¼ cup butter
- ½ cup dry bread crumbs

1. In a Dutch oven, slowly bring the chicken and water to a boil. Cover and simmer for 45-60 minutes or until chicken is tender, skimming the surface as foam rises.
2. Remove chicken and set aside until cool enough to handle. Remove and discard skin and bones. Cube chicken and return to broth.
3. Add the potatoes, onions, beans and seasonings. Bring to a boil. Reduce heat; simmer, uncovered, for 30 minutes or until potatoes are tender. Stir in remaining ingredients. Simmer, uncovered, for 10 minutes or until slightly thickened.

CHEESY TORTILLA SOUP

BRUNSWICK STEW

Cheesy Tortilla Soup

My daughter came up with this dish when trying to duplicate a soup she sampled at a restaurant. I always tell her how much people like it when I serve it.

—LAVONDA OWEN MARLOW, OK

PREP: 10 MIN. + MARINATING • **COOK:** 15 MIN.
MAKES: 8 SERVINGS (2 QUARTS)

- 1 envelope chicken fajita seasoning mix
- 1 pound boneless skinless chicken breasts, diced
- 2 tablespoons canola oil
- ½ cup chopped onion
- ¼ cup butter, cubed
- ⅓ cup all-purpose flour
- 2 cans (14½ ounces each) chicken broth
- ⅓ cup canned diced tomatoes with chilies
- 1 cup cubed process cheese (Velveeta)
- 1½ cups (6 ounces) shredded Monterey Jack cheese, divided
- 1½ cups half-and-half cream
- ½ cup shredded cheddar cheese
  Guacamole and tortilla chips

1. Prepare fajita mix according to package directions; add chicken and marinate as directed. In a large skillet, cook chicken in oil until no longer pink; set aside.
2. In a large saucepan, saute onion in butter until tender. Stir in flour until blended. Gradually stir in broth. Bring to a boil. Cook and stir for 2 minutes or until thickened and bubbly. Add the tomatoes, process cheese and 1 cup Monterey Jack; cook and stir until cheese is melted.
3. Stir in cream and reserved chicken; heat through (do not boil). Sprinkle with cheddar and remaining Monterey Jack cheese; top with guacamole and chips.

White Chili

Folks will enjoy a change from the traditional when they spoon into this flavorful blend of tender chunks of chicken, white beans and just enough spice.

—TASTE OF HOME COOKING SCHOOL

PREP: 15 MIN. • **COOK:** 25 MIN. • **MAKES:** 10 SERVINGS (2½ QUARTS)

- 1 **pound boneless skinless chicken breasts, chopped**
- 1 **medium onion, chopped**
- 1 **tablespoon olive oil**
- 2 **garlic cloves, minced**
- 2 **cans (14 ounces each) chicken broth**
- 1 **can (4 ounces) chopped green chilies**
- 2 **teaspoons ground cumin**
- 2 **teaspoons dried oregano**
- 1½ **teaspoons cayenne pepper**
- 3 **cans (14½ ounces each) great northern beans, drained, divided**
- 1 **cup (4 ounces) shredded Monterey Jack cheese**
  Chopped jalapeno pepper, optional

1. In a Dutch oven over medium heat, cook chicken and onion in oil until lightly browned. Add garlic; cook 1 minute longer. Stir in the broth, chilies, cumin, oregano and cayenne; bring to a boil.

2. Reduce heat to low. With a potato masher, mash one can of beans until smooth. Add to saucepan. Add remaining beans to saucepan. Simmer for 20-30 minutes or until chicken is no longer pink and onion is tender.

3. Top each serving with cheese and jalapeno pepper if desired.

CHUNKY CHICKEN NOODLE SOUP

SERVES 2

Chunky Chicken Noodle Soup

When winter holds me in its icy grip, I rely on this hearty, old-fashioned chicken soup to warm me right down to my toes. It's just like Grandma used to make—full of veggies and rich flavor.

—SHARON SKILDUM MAPLE GROVE, MN

START TO FINISH: 25 MIN. **MAKES:** 2 SERVINGS

- ¼ **cup diced carrot**
- 2 **tablespoons diced celery**
- 2 **tablespoons chopped onion**
- 1 **teaspoon butter**
- 2½ **cups reduced-sodium chicken broth**
- ⅔ **cup diced cooked chicken**
- ¼ **teaspoon salt**
- ¼ **teaspoon dried marjoram**
- ¼ **teaspoon dried thyme**
  Dash pepper
- ½ **cup uncooked medium egg noodles**
- 1 **teaspoon minced fresh parsley**

In a large saucepan, saute the carrot, celery and onion in butter until tender. Stir in the broth, chicken and seasonings; bring to a boil. Reduce heat. Add noodles; cook for 10 minutes or until tender. Sprinkle with parsley.

WHITE CHILI

Greek Chicken Soup is my go-to soup when I'm under the weather. It always makes me feel better!

—ANGIE PITTS CHARLESTON, SC

Greek Chicken Soup

MEXICAN CHICKEN SOUP
WITH CILANTRO DUMPLINGS

PREP: 25 MIN. • **COOK:** 40 MIN.
MAKES: 8 SERVINGS (2 QUARTS)

- 1½ pounds boneless skinless chicken breasts, cut into ¾-inch cubes
- 1 tablespoon Greek seasoning
- 1 teaspoon pepper
- 1 tablespoon olive oil
- 4 green onions, thinly sliced
- 1 garlic clove, minced
- ¼ cup white wine or chicken broth
- 7 cups reduced-sodium chicken broth
- ¼ cup chopped sun-dried tomatoes (not packed in oil)
- ¼ cup pitted Greek olives, sliced
- 1 tablespoon capers, drained
- 1½ teaspoons minced fresh basil or ½ teaspoon dried basil
- 1½ teaspoons minced fresh oregano or ½ teaspoon dried oregano
- 1½ cups uncooked orzo pasta
- 2 tablespoons lemon juice
- 1½ teaspoons minced fresh parsley

1. Season chicken with Greek seasoning and pepper. In a Dutch oven, saute chicken in oil until no longer pink; remove and set aside. Add green onions and garlic to the pan; saute for 1 minute. Add wine, stirring to loosen browned bits from pan.
2. Stir in the broth, tomatoes, olives, capers, basil, oregano and chicken. Bring to a boil. Reduce heat; cover and simmer for 15 minutes. Return to a boil. Stir in orzo. Cook 8-10 minutes longer or until pasta is tender. Stir in lemon juice and parsley.

 **Did you know?**
The spoon was invented in Europe during the 17th century to accommodate the giant ruffles that people wore around their necks. This made eating soup much easier!

Mexican Chicken Soup with Cilantro Dumplings

I just had to share this recipe because my whole family thought it was absolutely delicious! It's a filling and comforting twist on traditional chicken soup.
—**JENNY DUBINSKY** INWOOD, WV

PREP: 20 MIN. • **COOK:** 40 MIN.
MAKES: 6 SERVINGS
(2¼ QUARTS PLUS 12 DUMPLINGS)

- 1 pound boneless skinless chicken breasts, cut into 1-inch cubes
- 2 teaspoons olive oil, divided
- 1 medium onion, chopped
- 1 tablespoon chili powder
- 5 cups reduced-sodium chicken broth
- 1 can (15½ ounces) petite diced tomatoes, undrained
- 1 can (15 ounces) black beans, rinsed and drained
- 2 cups frozen corn
- 1 jalapeno pepper, seeded and minced
- 1 cup reduced-fat biscuit/baking mix
- ¼ cup minced fresh cilantro
- ¼ teaspoon ground cumin
- ⅓ cup fat-free milk

1. In a Dutch oven, saute chicken in 1 teaspoon oil until no longer pink. Remove and keep warm.
2. In the same pan, saute onion and chili powder in remaining oil until onion is tender. Add the broth, tomatoes, beans, corn and jalapeno. Bring to a boil. Reduce heat; cover and simmer for 20 minutes. Stir in reserved chicken.
3. In a small bowl, combine the biscuit mix, cilantro and cumin. Stir in milk just until moistened. Drop by tablespoonfuls onto simmering soup. Cover and simmer for 15 minutes or until a toothpick inserted in a dumpling comes out clean.

Chicken and Sweet Potato Chili

Sweet potatoes and chicken make this chili a meal in one bowl. But because it's thick, I sometimes spoon it over rice and serve it with cornmeal rolls.

—BRYNN RADER OLYMPIA, WA

PREP: 35 MIN. • **COOK:** 1½ HOURS
MAKES: 10 SERVINGS (3½ QUARTS)

- 1 **medium onion, chopped**
- 1 **whole garlic bulb, cloves separated, peeled and minced**
- 2 **tablespoons olive oil**
- 1 **broiler/fryer chicken (3 to 4 pounds), cut up**
- 2 **cans (14½ ounces each) plus 1½ cups chicken broth, divided**
- 1 **tablespoon chili powder**
- ¾ **teaspoon salt**
- ¼ **teaspoon crushed red pepper flakes**
- ¼ **teaspoon pepper**
- ½ **cup quinoa, rinsed**
- 3 **medium sweet potatoes, peeled and cubed**
- 2 **cans (15 ounces each) black beans, rinsed and drained**
- 2 **cans (16 ounces each) kidney beans, rinsed and drained**
- 1 **can (14½ ounces) diced tomatoes, undrained**

1. In a Dutch oven, saute onion and garlic in oil until tender. Add the chicken, 2 cans broth and seasonings. Bring to a boil. Reduce heat; cover and simmer for 1 hour or until chicken is tender.

2. Meanwhile, in a small saucepan, bring remaining broth to a boil. Add quinoa. Reduce heat; cover and simmer for 12-15 minutes or until liquid is absorbed. Remove from the heat; fluff with a fork. Set aside.

3. Remove chicken; cool slightly. Strain broth, reserving vegetables; skim fat from broth. Return vegetables and broth to the Dutch oven; add the sweet potatoes, beans, tomatoes and cooked quinoa. Bring to a boil. Reduce heat; simmer for 15-20 minutes or until sweet potatoes are tender.

4. Meanwhile, remove chicken from bones; cut into bite-size pieces. Discard bones. Stir chicken into chili; heat through.

TUSCAN CHICKEN SOUP

Tuscan Chicken Soup

Change up your traditional chicken soup by adding white kidney beans. You can use no-salt-added beans and reduced-sodium chicken broth to lower the sodium in this nutrient-rich soup.

—ROSEMARY GOETZ HUDSON, NY

PREP: 15 MIN. • **COOK:** 20 MIN.
MAKES: 4 SERVINGS

- 1 **small onion, chopped**
- 1 **small carrot, sliced**
- 1 **tablespoon olive oil**
- 2 **cans (14½ ounces each) chicken broth**
- 1 **cup water**
- ¾ **teaspoon salt**
- ¼ **teaspoon pepper**
- 1 **can (15 ounces) white kidney or cannellini beans, rinsed and drained**
- ⅔ **cup uncooked small spiral pasta**
- 3 **cups thinly sliced fresh escarole or spinach**
- 2 **cups shredded cooked chicken**

1. In a large saucepan, saute onion and carrot in oil until onion is tender. Add the broth, water, salt and pepper; bring to a boil. Stir in beans and pasta; return to a boil.

2. Reduce heat; cover and simmer for 15 minutes or until pasta and vegetables are tender, stirring occasionally. Add escarole and chicken; heat through.

CHICKEN AND SWEET POTATO CHILI

Stocks and broths are made by simmering meats, poultry, fish and/or vegetables, and make delicious bases for soups and other recipes. This easy method will leave you with 2 quarts of homemade Chicken Broth.

❶ Remove the excess fat from the cut up chicken. In a kettle or Dutch oven, combine chicken, vegetables, cold water and seasonings.

❷ Bring to a boil over low heat. Skim foam as it rises to the top of the water. Reduce heat; cover and simmer until the chicken is tender, about 1 hour.

❸ Remove meat from stock. Line a colander with a double thickness of cheesecloth; place in a large heat-resistant bowl. Pour stock into colander. Discard vegetables, seasonings and cheesecloth.

❹ Once chicken is cool enough to handle, remove meat from bones; discard skin and bones. Dice chicken; use immediately or cover and refrigerate. Chill broth several hours or overnight; lift fat from surface and discard. At this point, you can make soup or store broth in fridge for 3 days or freeze up to 6 months.

To make chicken noodle soup:
Place broth and desired veggies in a large saucepan. Bring to a boil, reduce heat, cover and simmer for 10 minutes. Add uncooked egg noodles and reserved cooked chicken. Bring to boil, reduce heat, cover and simmer for 6-10 minutes until noodles are tender.

Chicken Broth

Use this simple recipe to make an easy homemade chicken broth. The broth can be refrigerated for 3 days or frozen for up to 6 months.

—**NILA GRAHL** GURNEE, IL

PREP: 25 MIN. • **COOK:** 1½ HOURS
MAKES: ABOUT 2 QUARTS

 1 **broiler/fryer chicken (3 to 4 pounds), cut up**
10 **cups water**
 1 **large carrot, sliced**
 1 **large onion, sliced**
 1 **celery rib, sliced**
 1 **garlic clove, minced**
 1 **bay leaf**
 1 **teaspoon dried thyme**
 1 **teaspoon salt**
 ¼ **teaspoon pepper**

1. In a stockpot, combine all the ingredients. Slowly bring to a boil over low heat. Cover and simmer 45-60 minutes or until the meat is tender, skimming the surface as foam rises.
2. Remove chicken and set aside until cool enough to handle. Remove and discard skin and bones. Chop chicken; set aside for soup or save for another use.
3. Strain broth through a cheesecloth-lined colander, discarding vegetables and bay leaf. If using immediately, skim fat or refrigerate 8 hours or overnight; remove fat from surface. Broth can be covered and refrigerated up to 3 days or frozen 4 to 6 months.

top tip Salting Soups

Avoid adding salt, as well as other flavors, when making stock since it concentrates as it simmers and the liquid evaporates. Taste the soup when it's about ready to be served and add just enough salt to suit your family's preference.

**SPICY CHICKEN
TOMATO PITAS**
PAGE 28

Salads& Sandwiches

Curried Chicken Rice Salad

Since I usually make and serve this salad while my teacher friends and I are on summer break, I always associate this recipe with relaxed good times! It's best to make ahead so that the flavors can mingle.

—PAMELA HESSELBART SYLVANIA, OH

PREP: 50 MIN. + CHILLING
MAKES: 6 SERVINGS

- 1 package (6.6 ounces) toasted almond rice pilaf
- 2 cups cubed cooked chicken
- ¾ cup diced celery
- ½ cup dried cranberries
- ½ cup golden raisins
- ½ cup mayonnaise
- ⅓ cup chutney
- 3 tablespoons sour cream
- 2 tablespoons lemon juice
- 1 teaspoon curry powder
- 2 medium apples, cubed
- 8 lettuce leaves
- ¼ cup sliced almonds, toasted

1. Cook rice pilaf according to package directions; cool. In a large bowl, combine the chicken, celery, cranberries, raisins and rice.
2. In a small bowl, combine the mayonnaise, chutney, sour cream, lemon juice and curry powder; stir in apples. Add to rice mixture; toss to coat. Cover and refrigerate for at least 2 hours.
3. Serve on lettuce; garnish with almonds.

CURRIED CHICKEN RICE SALAD

Grilled Chicken Salad with Blueberry Vinaigrette

A scrumptious combo of spring colors, textures and fresh flavors come together in this easy main-dish salad. I enjoy it with a fresh baguette and a frosty glass of minted lemonade.

—SUSAN GAUTHIER FALMOUTH, ME

PREP: 20 MIN. + MARINATING
GRILL: 10 MIN. • **MAKES:** 4 SERVINGS

- 3 tablespoons olive oil
- 1 garlic clove, minced
- 1 teaspoon salt
- 1 teaspoon pepper
- 2 boneless skinless chicken breast halves (6 ounces each)

VINAIGRETTE
- ¼ cup olive oil
- ¼ cup blueberry preserves
- 2 tablespoons maple syrup
- 2 tablespoons balsamic vinegar
- ¼ teaspoon ground mustard
- ⅛ teaspoon salt
  Dash pepper

SALADS
- 1 package (10 ounces) ready-to-serve salad greens
- 1 cup fresh blueberries
- 1 snack-size cup (4 ounces) mandarin oranges, drained
- 1 cup crumbled goat cheese

1. In a large resealable plastic bag, combine the oil, garlic, salt and pepper; add the chicken. Seal bag and turn to coat; refrigerate for 30 minutes.
2. In a small bowl, whisk vinaigrette ingredients. Cover and refrigerate until ready to use.
3. Drain and discard marinade. Grill chicken, covered, over medium heat for 5-7 minutes on each side or until a meat thermometer reads 160°. When cool enough to handle, cut chicken into slices.
4. Divide salad greens among four serving plates. Top each with chicken, blueberries and oranges. Whisk vinaigrette and drizzle over salads; sprinkle with cheese.

CHICKEN CAESAR
BURGERS

SERVES ②

Chicken Caesar Burgers

I sometimes make these burgers with ground turkey, depending on what's cheaper. Either way, it's a delicious, lean option that will satisfy any burger craving.
—**RACHEL RICCOMINI** SAINT MARYS, KS

START TO FINISH: 30 MIN.
MAKES: 2 SERVINGS

- ¼ **cup finely chopped onion**
- 2 **tablespoons shredded Parmesan cheese, divided**
- 1 **tablespoon lemon juice**
- 1½ **teaspoons dried parsley flakes**
- 1 **garlic clove, minced**
- 1 **teaspoon Worcestershire sauce**
- ¼ **teaspoon salt**
- ¼ **teaspoon pepper**
- ½ **pound ground chicken**
- 2 **hamburger buns, split**
- ¼ **cup torn romaine**
- 4 **teaspoons fat-free creamy Caesar salad dressing**

1. In a small bowl, combine the onion, 1 tablespoon cheese, lemon juice, parsley, garlic, Worcestershire sauce, salt and pepper. Crumble chicken over mixture and mix well. Shape into two patties.
2. Grill burgers, covered, over medium heat for 5-7 minutes on each side or until a meat thermometer reads 165° and juices run clear. Sprinkle with remaining cheese.
3. Serve on buns with romaine and salad dressing.

Open-Faced Chicken Avocado Burgers

A creamy avocado spread and thick slices of fresh mozzarella and tomato dress up these chicken patties. I serve them with boiled potatoes and a bit of butter.
—**LISA HUNDLEY** ABERDEEN, NC

PREP: 30 MIN. • **COOK:** 15 MIN.
MAKES: 4 SERVINGS
PLUS ¼ CUP LEFTOVER SPREAD

- 1 **tablespoon lemon juice**
- ¼ **teaspoon Worcestershire sauce**
- ½ **medium ripe avocado, peeled**
- ½ **cup mayonnaise**
- ¼ **cup sour cream**
- 4 **green onions, coarsely chopped**
- ½ **teaspoon salt**
- ½ **teaspoon cayenne pepper**

BURGERS

- ¼ **cup shredded Parmesan cheese**
- 2 **tablespoons prepared pesto**
- 3 **garlic cloves, minced**
- ¼ **teaspoon salt**
- 1 **pound ground chicken**
- 4 **tablespoons olive oil, divided**
- ½ **pound fresh mozzarella cheese, cut into 4 slices**
- 4 **slices Italian bread (¾ inch thick)**
- 2 **cups fresh arugula or baby spinach**
- 8 **slices tomato**
- ¼ **teaspoon dried basil**
- ¼ **teaspoon pepper**

1. In a blender, combine the first eight ingredients; cover and process until smooth. Chill until serving. For burgers, in a small bowl, combine the Parmesan cheese, pesto, garlic and salt. Crumble chicken over mixture and mix well. Shape into four patties.
2. In a large skillet over medium heat, cook burgers in 2 tablespoons oil for 5-7 minutes on each side or until a thermometer reads 165° and juices run clear. Top with cheese; cover and cook 1 minute longer.
3. Meanwhile, brush bread with remaining oil; place on a baking sheet. Broil 3-4 in. from the heat for 1-2 minutes on each side or until toasted.
4. Spread each slice of toast with 2 tablespoons avocado spread (refrigerate remaining spread for another use). Top with arugula, a burger and sliced tomato. Sprinkle with basil and pepper.

OPEN-FACED CHICKEN
AVOCADO BURGER

SALADS & SANDWICHES

Spicy Chicken Tomato Pitas

I'm not sure if this is a Mediterranean dish with a Southwestern flair or the other way around. All I know is that it's ideal for a summer dinner. The tomato relish is yummy as an appetizer with tortilla chips, so you may want to double it.

—**CORI COOPER** BOISE, ID

START TO FINISH: 30 MIN. • **MAKES:** 4 SERVINGS

TOMATO RELISH
- ¼ **cup lemon juice**
- 1 **tablespoon olive oil**
- 1 **teaspoon ground coriander**
- 1 **teaspoon ground cumin**
- ¼ **teaspoon crushed red pepper flakes**
- 4 **medium tomatoes, seeded and chopped**
- 1 **small onion, chopped**
- ¼ **cup minced fresh parsley**

CHICKEN PITAS
- 1 **tablespoon ground cumin**
- 1 **tablespoon paprika**
- 1½ **teaspoons dried oregano**
- 1½ **teaspoons ground coriander**
- ½ **teaspoon crushed red pepper flakes**
- ¼ **teaspoon salt**
- 4 **boneless skinless chicken breast halves (4 ounces each)**
- 8 **whole wheat pita pocket halves**

1. In a bowl, whisk the first five ingredients. Add tomatoes, onion and parsley; toss to coat. Refrigerate until serving.
2. Moisten a paper towel with cooking oil; using long-handled tongs, rub on grill rack to coat lightly. Combine cumin, paprika, oregano, coriander, pepper flakes and salt; rub onto both sides of chicken. Grill chicken, covered, over medium heat or broil 4 in. from heat 4-7 minutes on each side or until a thermometer reads 165°.
3. Cut chicken into slices. Serve in pita halves with relish.

SPICY CHICKEN
TOMATO PITAS

Chicken Pesto Sandwiches

These easy sandwiches are great for game day! They're tasty, and also so easy to prep ahead and assemble later at the event.

—**COLLEEN STURMA** MILWAUKEE, WI

START TO FINISH: 30 MIN.. • **MAKES:** 6 SERVINGS

- 6 **boneless skinless chicken breast halves (4 ounces each)**
- ¾ **cup prepared pesto, divided**
- ½ **teaspoon salt**
- ¼ **teaspoon pepper**
- 12 **slices Italian bread (½ inch thick), toasted**
- 1 **jar (12 ounces) roasted sweet red peppers, drained**
- ¼ **pound fresh mozzarella cheese, cut into six slices**

1. Flatten chicken to ¼-in. thickness. Spread 1 tablespoon pesto over each chicken breast; sprinkle with salt and pepper. Grill chicken, covered, over medium heat for 3-5 minutes on each side or until no longer pink.
2. Spread 3 tablespoons pesto over six slices of toast; layer with red peppers, chicken and cheese. Spread remaining pesto over remaining toast; place over top.

1. For dressing, in a small bowl, whisk the first nine ingredients until smooth; set aside.
2. In a large saucepan, cook spaghetti according to package directions, adding the carrots during the last 2 minutes of cooking; drain. Transfer to a large bowl; stir in cabbage and chicken.
3. Whisk dressing and pour over spaghetti mixture; toss to coat. Sprinkle with cilantro and peanuts. Serve immediately or chill before serving.

Honey-Mustard Chicken Sandwiches

These sandwiches have a sweet tang from the honey mustard, but I like to add extra cayenne to give them a kick of heat.
—**CHRISTINA LEVRANT** HENDERSON, NV

START TO FINISH: 20 MIN. • **MAKES:** 4 SERVINGS

- ¼ cup **Dijon mustard**
- 2 tablespoons **honey**
- 1 teaspoon **dried oregano**
- 1 teaspoon **water**
- ¼ teaspoon **garlic powder**
- ⅛ to ¼ teaspoon **cayenne pepper**
- 4 **boneless skinless chicken breast halves** (4 ounces each)
- 4 **sandwich buns, split**
- 1 cup **shredded lettuce**
- 8 **thin tomato slices**

In a small bowl, combine the first six ingredients. Broil chicken 4 in. from the heat for 4-7 minutes on each side or until a meat thermometer reads 170°, brushing occasionally with mustard mixture. Serve on buns with lettuce and tomato.

> My husband considers this one of his favorite recipes. We call them peanut butter noodles. The dressing is also good served hot on stir-fried chicken and veggies —**BETH DAUENHAUER** PUEBLO, CO

THAI CHICKEN PASTA SALAD

Thai Chicken Pasta Salad

START TO FINISH: 30 MIN. • **MAKES:** 8 SERVINGS

- ¾ cup **reduced-fat creamy peanut butter**
- 3 tablespoons **water**
- 3 tablespoons **lime juice**
- 3 tablespoons **molasses**
- 4½ teaspoons **reduced-sodium soy sauce**
- 3 **garlic cloves, minced**
- 1½ teaspoons **rice vinegar**
- 1½ teaspoons **sesame oil**
- ¼ teaspoon **crushed red pepper flakes**

SALAD
- 12 ounces **uncooked whole wheat spaghetti**
- 2 large **carrots, julienned**
- 8 cups **finely shredded Chinese or napa cabbage**
- 2 cups **shredded cooked chicken breast**
- ⅔ cup **minced fresh cilantro**
- 3 tablespoons **unsalted dry roasted peanuts, chopped**

HONEY-MUSTARD
CHICKEN SANDWICHES

CARIBBEAN CHICKEN
CAESAR SALAD

Caribbean Chicken Caesar Salad

A friend of mine loved the food served at her wedding reception. Afterward, we re-created the menu, including this salad with its refreshing citrus accent.

—**BARBARA CARLUCCI** ORANGE PARK, FL

START TO FINISH: 30 MIN.
MAKES: 4 SERVINGS

- 1 **pound boneless skinless chicken breasts, cut into 1-inch pieces**
- ½ **cup thawed non-alcoholic pina colada mix, divided**
- 1 **cup tangerine or mandarin orange segments**
- 1 **celery rib, chopped**
- 2 **tablespoons crushed pineapple**
- 1 **green onion, chopped**
- 4 **pitted ripe olives, sliced**
- 2 **tablespoons plus 2 teaspoons lemon juice**
- 4 **teaspoons mayonnaise**
- 2 **teaspoons grated Parmesan cheese**
- 1 **to 2 garlic cloves, minced**
- ⅛ **teaspoon salt**
- ⅛ **teaspoon pepper**
- 4 **cups torn romaine or iceberg lettuce**

1. Combine chicken and ¼ cup pina colada mix. In a large skillet coated with cooking spray, cook and stir chicken mixture over medium heat until chicken is no longer pink. Remove from the heat; set aside.
2. Combine the tangerines, celery, pineapple, onion and olives in a large bowl. In a small bowl, combine the lemon juice, mayonnaise, cheese, garlic, salt, pepper and the remaining pina colada mix.
3. Add chicken and romaine to the tangerine mixture; drizzle with dressing and toss to coat.

 Did you know?
The original Caesar salad was eaten with your fingers instead of a fork. Romaine lettuce leaves were arranged with the stems facing out, and each piece had all the ingredients on top of it.

GRILLED PEPPER JACK CHICKEN SANDWICHES

SERVES 2

Grilled Pepper Jack Chicken Sandwiches

I think this is the perfect meal for two to enjoy with some grilled fries on a summer day. Even with bacon and cheese, these sandwiches have less than 350 calories.

—**LINDA FOREMAN** LOCUST GROVE, OK

START TO FINISH: 25 MIN.
MAKES: 2 SERVINGS

- 2 **boneless skinless chicken breast halves (4 ounces each)**
- 1 **teaspoon poultry seasoning**
- 2 **center-cut bacon strips, cooked and halved**
- 2 **slices (½ ounce each) pepper Jack cheese**
- 2 **hamburger buns, split**
- 2 **lettuce leaves**
- 1 **slice onion, separated into rings**
- 2 **slices tomato**
  Dill pickle slices, optional

1. Sprinkle chicken with poultry seasoning. Moisten a paper towel with cooking oil; using long-handled tongs, lightly coat the grill rack.
2. Grill chicken, covered, over medium heat or broil 4 in. from the heat for 4-7 minutes on each side or until a thermometer reads 170°. Top with bacon and cheese; cover and cook 1-2 minutes longer or until cheese is melted.
3. Serve on buns with lettuce, onion, tomato and pickles if desired.

Southwest Chicken Salad

My husband loves salads, and this flavorful chicken recipe is easy, nutritious and very tasty. Serve it over greens, tucked in a pita or rolled up in a tortilla.

—**SARA HOBBS** QUINLAN, TX

START TO FINISH: 30 MIN. • **MAKES:** 6 CUPS

- 4 cups cubed rotisserie chicken
- 2 cups frozen corn, thawed
- 1 cup chopped roasted sweet red peppers
- 1 cup chopped red or sweet onion
- 1 cup minced fresh cilantro

DRESSING
- 3 tablespoons lime juice
- 3 tablespoons olive oil
- 4 teaspoons honey
- 2 teaspoons ground cumin
- 1 teaspoon salt
- 1 teaspoon chili powder
- ½ teaspoon coarsely ground pepper

In a large bowl, combine the first five ingredients. In a small bowl, whisk the dressing ingredients; pour over chicken mixture and toss to coat. Refrigerate until serving.

GREEK CHICKEN
SANDWICHES

Greek Chicken Sandwiches

My wife and I ate sandwiches similar to these at a restaurant and enjoyed them. But they weren't nearly as flavorful as the easy recipe I came up with to re-create them.

—**TOM WOLF** TIGARD, OR

START TO FINISH: 25 MIN. • **MAKES:** 4 SERVINGS

- 1 pound boneless skinless chicken breasts, cut into 1-inch cubes
- ⅓ cup fat-free creamy Caesar salad dressing
- ¼ cup crumbled feta cheese
- ¼ cup pitted Greek olives, finely chopped
- ¼ teaspoon garlic powder
- 8 pita pocket halves
- 8 lettuce leaves
- 1 medium tomato, sliced
- 1 small onion, sliced

1. In a large nonstick skillet coated with cooking spray, cook and stir chicken over medium heat until no longer pink. Add the dressing, cheese, olives and garlic powder; heat through.

2. Line pita halves with lettuce, tomato and onion; fill each with about ⅓ cup chicken mixture.

SOUTHWEST
CHICKEN SALAD

Berry Chicken Salad

People either love or hate the distinct flavor of goat cheese. If you're a fan, try it with this berry-studded chicken salad. If not, feta cheese works great, too.
—**WENDY BALL** BATTLE CREEK, MI

START TO FINISH: 20 MIN. • **MAKES:** 4 SERVINGS

- 4 boneless skinless chicken breast halves (4 ounces each)
- ¼ teaspoon salt
- ¼ teaspoon pepper
- 1 package (6 ounces) fresh baby spinach
- 1 cup fresh raspberries
- 1 cup halved fresh strawberries
- ⅔ cup crumbled goat cheese
- 3 tablespoons chopped pecans, toasted
- ¼ cup prepared fat-free raspberry vinaigrette

1. Sprinkle chicken with salt and pepper. Grill chicken, covered, over medium heat or broil 4 in. from the heat for 4-7 minutes on each side or until juices run clear.
2. In a large bowl, combine the spinach, raspberries, strawberries, cheese and pecans. Divide among four serving plates. Slice chicken and arrange over spinach mixture; drizzle with vinaigrette.

BERRY CHICKEN SALAD

CASHEW CHICKEN SALAD SANDWICHES

Cashew Chicken Salad Sandwiches

I think this is the best chicken salad recipe around! It's good for you, has wonderful flavor and is quick to fix.
—**PEGGI KELLY** FAIRBURY, NE

START TO FINISH: 15 MIN. • **MAKES:** 6 SERVINGS

- 2 cups diced cooked chicken
- ½ cup chopped salted cashews
- ½ cup chopped red apple
- ½ cup chopped peeled cucumber
- ½ cup mayonnaise
- ½ teaspoon sugar
- ½ teaspoon salt
  Dash pepper
- 6 lettuce leaves, optional
- 6 kaiser rolls or croissants, split

1. In a large bowl, combine the chicken, cashews, apple and cucumber. In a small bowl, combine the mayonnaise, sugar, salt and pepper. Add to chicken mixture and toss to coat.
2. Place a lettuce leaf if desired and ½ cup chicken salad on each roll bottom; replace tops.

top tip

Chicken Salad Bake

After a party, I had lots of leftover chicken salad. I mixed it with cream of chicken soup, chopped sweet red pepper and crushed Triscuit crackers. I put it in a casserole dish and baked it at 350° for about 25 minutes. Then I topped it with more crushed Triscuits and baked it for 10 minutes longer. It was fantastic! —**TRICIA JOHNSTON** ATLANTA, GA

TUSCAN CHICKEN
PAGE 43

Stovetop Suppers

{ **CHICKEN PESTO
WITH PASTA**
PAGE 40 }

{ **CREAMY CHICKEN
TORTELLINI**
PAGE 51 }

{ **CHICKEN AND
SAUSAGE PENNE**
PAGE 57 }

I had paella for the first time in Spain. It was so good, I've been on a quest to re-create the rich flavors of that dish ever since. We love the shrimp, chicken, veggie and olives in this easy make-at-home version.

—LIBBY WALP CHICAGO, IL

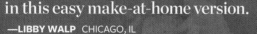

HEARTY PAELLA

1. In a large skillet over medium heat, cook chicken in oil until no longer pink. Remove and keep warm. Add rice and onion to the pan; cook until rice is lightly browned and onion is tender, stirring frequently. Add garlic; cook 1 minute longer.

2. Stir in the broth, tomatoes, oregano, paprika, salt, pepper, saffron and turmeric. Bring to a boil. Reduce heat to low; cover and cook for 10 minutes.

3. Add the shrimp, peas and olives. Cover and cook 10 minutes longer or until rice is tender, shrimp turns pink and liquid is absorbed. Add chicken; heat through. Serve with lemon wedges.

Cashew Chicken

My mom loves Chinese food. This easy recipe helps satisfy her craving when carry-out is not available.

—RICK SHAW GAINESVILLE, GA

START TO FINISH: 30 MIN.
MAKES: 4 SERVINGS

- 4 teaspoons cornstarch
- 2 teaspoons sugar
- ½ cup cold water
- ⅓ cup soy sauce
- 2 teaspoons minced fresh gingerroot
- 1 teaspoon crushed red pepper flakes
- 1⅓ pounds boneless skinless chicken breasts, cut into 1-inch strips
- 2 tablespoons canola oil
- 2 celery ribs, chopped
- 2 medium carrots, chopped
- 1 medium onion, chopped
- 1 cup whole salted cashews
  Hot cooked rice, optional

1. In a small bowl, combine the first six ingredients; set aside.

2. In a large skillet or wok, stir-fry chicken in oil until no longer pink. Remove and keep warm. In the same pan, stir-fry the celery, carrots and onion until crisp-tender.

3. Stir cornstarch mixture and add to the pan. Bring to a boil; cook and stir for 2 minutes or until thickened. Add chicken and cashews; heat through. Serve with rice if desired.

Hearty Paella

PREP: 25 MIN. • **COOK:** 30 MIN.
MAKES: 6 SERVINGS

- 1¼ pounds boneless skinless chicken breasts, cut into 1-inch cubes
- 1 tablespoon olive oil
- 1 cup uncooked long grain rice
- 1 medium onion, chopped
- 2 garlic cloves, minced
- 2¼ cups reduced-sodium chicken broth
- 1 can (14½ ounces) diced tomatoes, undrained
- 1 teaspoon dried oregano
- ½ teaspoon paprika
- ¼ teaspoon salt
- ¼ teaspoon pepper
- ⅛ teaspoon saffron threads
- ⅛ teaspoon ground turmeric
- 1 pound uncooked medium shrimp, peeled and deveined
- ¾ cup frozen peas
- 12 pimiento-stuffed olives
- 1 medium lemon, cut into six wedges

Almond Chicken Strips

Teaching mornings, I have the afternoons to experiment with many recipes. This chicken is just as good served cold for a late night snack, as it is served hot for dinner. Unfortunately, there are seldom any leftovers.
—WENDY THURSTON BOW ISLAND, AB

START TO FINISH: 25 MIN.
MAKES: 4 SERVINGS

- ¼ cup cornstarch
- 1 teaspoon sugar
- ½ teaspoon salt
- 4½ teaspoons sherry or chicken broth
- 2 egg whites, lightly beaten
- 1½ cups ground almonds
- 1 pound boneless skinless chicken breasts, cut into ½-inch strips
- 2 tablespoons canola oil
  Honey mustard, optional

1. In a shallow bowl, combine the cornstarch, sugar, salt and sherry; gradually stir in egg whites. Place almonds in another shallow bowl. Dip chicken in egg white mixture, then coat with almonds.
2. In a large skillet or wok, stir-fry chicken strips in oil for 5-7 minutes or until no longer pink; drain on paper towels. Serve with honey mustard for dipping if desired.

MAPLE PRETZEL CHICKEN

ALMOND CHICKEN STRIPS

Maple Pretzel Chicken

This unexpected combo delivers delicious results. The finer the pretzel crumb, the better. Larger pieces won't coat as well.
—TARA SZLAG COLUMBUS, OH

START TO FINISH: 20 MIN.
MAKES: 4 SERVINGS

- 4 boneless skinless chicken breast halves (5 ounces each)
- 1 egg
- ½ cup maple syrup
- 1½ cups crushed pretzels
- ¼ cup canola oil

1. Flatten chicken breasts to ½-in. thickness. In a shallow bowl, whisk egg and syrup. Place pretzels in a separate shallow bowl. Dip chicken in egg mixture and coat with pretzels.
2. In a large skillet, cook chicken in oil over medium heat for 4-5 minutes on each side or until juices run clear.

top tip
DIY Dijon Dipping Sauce

Whip up a quick dipping sauce by whisking together 3 tablespoons Dijon mustard, 2 tablespoons red wine vinegar, 2 tablespoons reduced-sodium soy sauce, 1 tablespoon sesame oil and 1 teaspoon hot pepper sauce. Double or triple the recipe as needed. Sauce will be thin.

Balsamic Chicken Fettuccine

Skip the marinara and serve noodles an elegant new way. Not only is our easy balsamic-infused entree a meal in itself, it makes a different twist on an Italian classic.

—TASTE OF HOME TEST KITCHEN

START TO FINISH: 25 MIN.
MAKES: 5 SERVINGS

- 8 ounces uncooked fettuccine
- 1½ pounds boneless skinless chicken breasts, cut into strips
- 2 tablespoons plus ½ cup balsamic vinaigrette, divided
- ½ pound sliced fresh mushrooms
- 1 medium red onion, chopped
- 2 cans (14½ ounces each) diced tomatoes, undrained
- 2 cups frozen broccoli florets
- ½ teaspoon Italian seasoning

1. Cook fettuccine according to package directions. Meanwhile, in a large skillet, saute chicken in 1 tablespoon vinaigrette until no longer pink. Remove and keep warm.
2. In the same skillet, saute mushrooms and onion in 1 tablespoon vinaigrette until tender. Add the tomatoes, broccoli, Italian seasoning and remaining vinaigrette; cook 5-6 minutes longer or until heated through.
3. Drain fettuccine. Add fettuccine and chicken to skillet and toss to coat.

BALSAMIC CHICKEN FETTUCCINE

FRIED CHICKEN WITH PAN GRAVY

Fried Chicken with Pan Gravy

Mom's traditional fried chicken always cooked up golden brown and crispy. Drizzled with the pan gravy, this dish is my ultimate comfort food.

—GINNY WERKMEISTER TILDEN, NE

PREP: 15 MIN. • **COOK:** 45 MIN.
MAKES: 6 SERVINGS (1½ CUPS GRAVY)

- 1 cup all-purpose flour
- ¾ teaspoon salt
- ¼ teaspoon dried thyme
- ¼ teaspoon rubbed sage
- ¼ teaspoon pepper
- 1 broiler/fryer chicken (3½ to 4 pounds), cut up
  Oil for frying

GRAVY
- 2 tablespoons all-purpose flour
- ⅛ teaspoon salt
- 1⅓ cups 2% milk

1. In a large resealable plastic bag, combine the first five ingredients. Add chicken, a few pieces at a time, and shake to coat.
2. In a large skillet over medium-high heat, heat ¼ in. of oil; fry chicken until browned on all sides. Reduce heat; cover and cook for 30-35 minutes or until juices run clear, turning occasionally. Uncover and cook 5 minutes longer. Remove chicken to paper towels and keep warm.
3. Pour off excess fat from the skillet, reserving the browned bits and 2 tablespoons drippings. Stir in flour and salt until blended; gradually add the milk. Bring to a boil; cook and stir for 1-2 minutes or until thickened. Serve with chicken.

HERBED FRIED CHICKEN WITH GRAVY *Omit sage. Add 1 teaspoon each dried tarragon, oregano, paprika and ground mustard, and ½ teaspoon each onion powder and garlic powder to the flour mixture. Proceed as directed.*

Parmesan Chicken Couscous

Simple ingredients make clever use of leftover chicken in an innovative dish any home cook would be proud to plate. I like to serve it with a side of fresh fruit.

—LISA ABBOTT NEW BERLIN, WI

START TO FINISH: 20 MIN.
MAKES: 4 SERVINGS

- ½ cup chopped walnuts
- 2 teaspoons olive oil, divided
- 3 garlic cloves, minced
- 2 cups chopped fresh spinach
- 1½ cups cubed cooked chicken
- 1¼ cups water
- 2 teaspoons dried basil
- ¼ teaspoon pepper
- 1 package (5.9 ounces) Parmesan couscous
- ¼ cup grated Parmesan cheese

1. In a large saucepan, cook walnuts over medium heat in 1 teaspoon oil for 2-3 minutes or until toasted. Remove and set aside.

2. In the same pan, saute garlic in remaining oil for 1 minute. Add the spinach, chicken, water, basil and pepper. Bring to a boil. Stir in couscous. Remove from the heat; cover and let stand for 5-10 minutes or until water is absorbed. Fluff with a fork. Stir in walnuts and sprinkle with cheese.

RUBY CHICKEN

PARMESAN CHICKEN COUSCOUS

SERVES ②

Ruby Chicken

I got this recipe when I went to the cranberry fest in Wisconsin in 1995. It's definitely a keeper. Even people who don't like cranberries like this dinner.

—KATHY MEAD GWINN, MI

PREP: 15 MIN. • **COOK:** 35 MIN.
MAKES: 2 SERVINGS

- 3 tablespoons all-purpose flour
- ¼ teaspoon salt
- 2 bone-in chicken breast halves (8 ounces each)
- 1 tablespoon butter
- ½ cup fresh or frozen cranberries
- ⅓ cup sugar
- ⅓ cup orange juice
- 2 tablespoons chopped onion
- ½ teaspoon grated orange peel
- ⅛ teaspoon ground ginger
- ⅛ teaspoon ground cinnamon

1. In a large resealable plastic bag, combine flour and salt; add the chicken. Seal bag and toss to coat. In a nonstick skillet, brown chicken in butter.

2. Meanwhile, in a small saucepan, combine the remaining ingredients. Bring to a boil over medium heat. Pour over chicken. Cover and simmer for 35-40 minutes or until a meat thermometer reads 170°.

Rubbing the chicken with spices enhances flavor but in less time than a liquid marinade. You can also save time by using pre-cut melon from the store.

—ROXANNE CHAN ALBANY, CA

CHICKEN BREASTS WITH
MELON RELISH

Lemon Teriyaki Chicken

My easy stovetop chicken features mild and delicate family-pleasing flavors. It's fantastic with rice and a green vegetable like broccoli.

—CLARA COULSON MINNEY
WASHINGTON COURT HOUSE, OH

START TO FINISH: 25 MIN.
MAKES: 4 SERVINGS

    4 boneless skinless chicken breast
       halves (4 ounces each)
    2 tablespoons all-purpose flour
    3 tablespoons butter
    ¼ cup reduced-sodium teriyaki sauce
    2 tablespoons lemon juice
    ¾ teaspoon minced garlic
    ½ teaspoon sugar

1. Flatten chicken to ½-in. thickness; coat with flour. In a large skillet, cook chicken in butter over medium heat for 4-5 minutes on each side or until a thermometer reads 170°. Remove and set aside.
2. Add the teriyaki sauce, lemon juice, garlic and sugar to the skillet; stir to loosen browned bits. Return chicken to the pan and heat through.

Chicken Pesto with Pasta

Keep a container of pesto in the freezer. The next time you have leftover chicken, whip up this simple pasta for dinner.

—TASTE OF HOME TEST KITCHEN

START TO FINISH: 20 MIN.
MAKES: 6 SERVINGS

    1 package (16 ounces) cellentani or
       spiral pasta
    2 cups cubed rotisserie chicken
    1 cup chopped fresh tomatoes
    1 container (7 ounces) prepared
       pesto
    ¼ cup pine nuts, toasted

Cook pasta according to package directions. Meanwhile, in a nonstick skillet, saute chicken and tomatoes for 2 minutes. Stir in pesto; heat through. Drain pasta; toss with chicken mixture. Sprinkle with pine nuts.

Chicken Breasts with Melon Relish

START TO FINISH: 30 MIN.
MAKES: 4 SERVINGS

    ¼ teaspoon salt
    ¼ teaspoon ground ginger
    ¼ teaspoon ground nutmeg
    ¼ teaspoon pepper
    4 boneless skinless chicken breast
       halves (6 ounces each)
    1 tablespoon canola oil
RELISH
    1 cup diced cantaloupe
    ¼ cup finely chopped celery
    1 green onion, chopped
    2 tablespoons minced fresh mint
    1 tablespoon chopped crystallized
       ginger
    1 tablespoon lime juice
    1 tablespoon honey
    ½ teaspoon grated lime peel

In a small bowl, combine salt, ginger, nutmeg and pepper. Rub over both sides of chicken. In a large skillet, cook chicken in oil over medium heat for 8-10 minutes on each side or until a meat thermometer reads 170°. Meanwhile, in a small bowl, combine relish ingredients. Serve with chicken.

CHICKEN PESTO
WITH PASTA

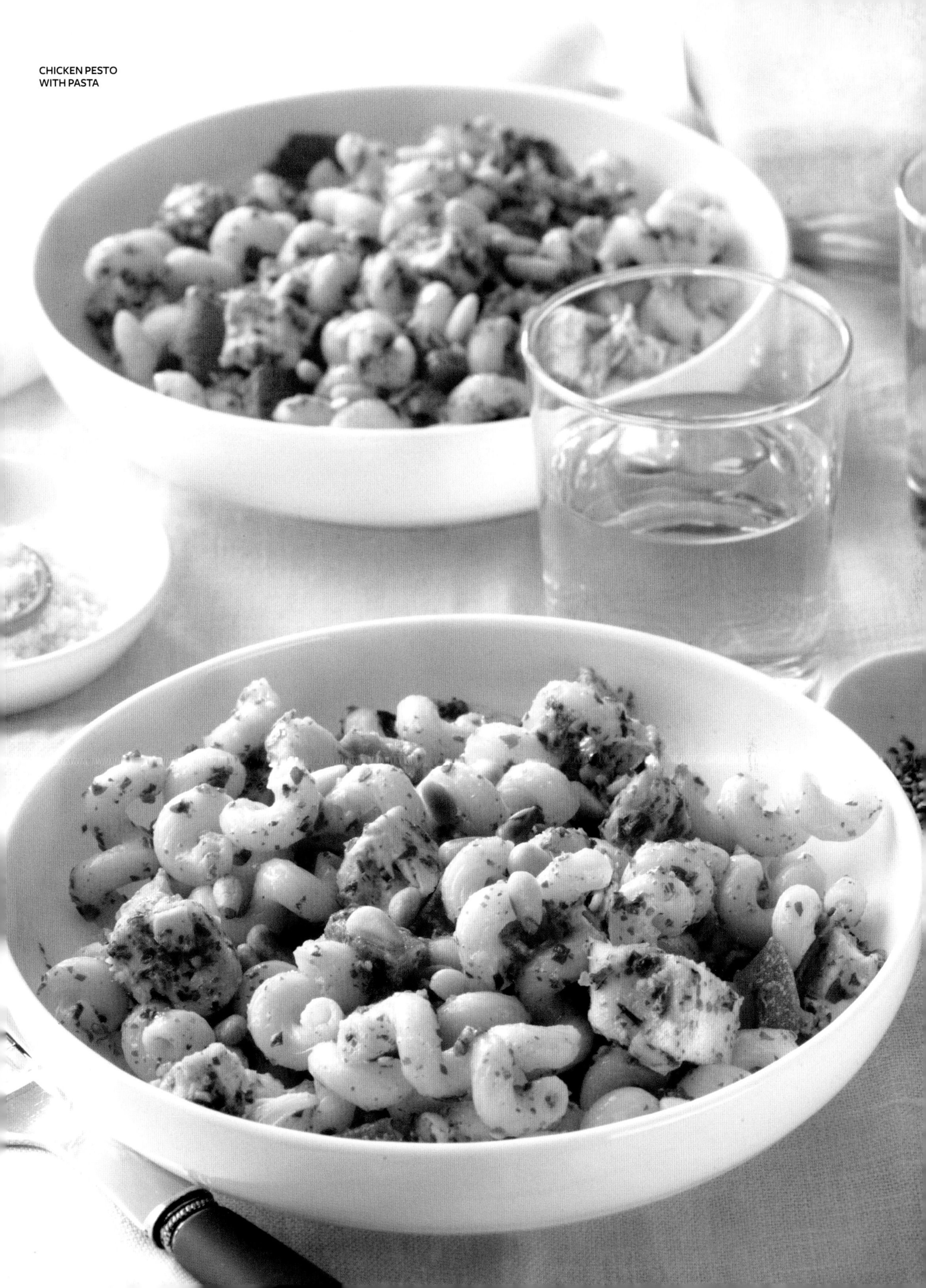

SERVES ②

Chicken Finger Tacos

Using chicken fingers in this recipe makes for the perfect size taco and also cuts down on prep time. I like to pair it with Spanish rice and refried beans for a complete meal for two.

—**KATHY WILLIAMS** I AYTON, UT

START TO FINISH: 20 MIN. • **MAKES:** 2 SERVINGS

- 1 egg, lightly beaten
- ½ cup seasoned bread crumbs
- ¼ teaspoon salt
- ⅛ teaspoon pepper
- 4 chicken tenderloins
- 1 tablespoon canola oil
- 4 corn tortillas (6 inches), warmed
- ½ cup shredded cheddar cheese
  Salsa, sour cream, guacamole, chopped tomatoes, shredded lettuce and fresh cilantro leaves, optional

1. Place egg in a shallow bowl. In another shallow bowl, combine the bread crumbs, salt and pepper. Dip chicken in egg, then roll in bread crumb mixture.
2. In a large skillet over medium heat, cook chicken in oil for 4-5 minutes on each side or until juices run clear. Serve on tortillas with cheese and optional ingredients if desired.

GREEK CHICKEN AND ARTICHOKES

CHICKEN FINGER TACOS

Greek Chicken and Artichokes

I'm a huge fan of wild rice and wild rice mixes. Try it in place of brown rice to add a nutty flavor to this dish.

—**CAITLIN CHANEY** TAMPA, FL

START TO FINISH: 30 MIN. • **MAKES:** 4 SERVINGS

- ¾ pound boneless skinless chicken breasts, cubed
- 1¼ teaspoons Greek seasoning
- 1 tablespoon olive oil
- 1 cup sliced fresh mushrooms
- 1 can (14½ ounces) no-salt-added diced tomatoes, undrained
- 1 can (14 ounces) water-packed artichoke hearts, rinsed, drained and quartered
- 2 cups cooked brown rice
- ¼ cup crumbled feta cheese

1. Sprinkle chicken with Greek seasoning. In a large skillet, brown chicken in oil. Add mushrooms; cook 2 minutes longer. Drain.
2. Stir in tomatoes and artichokes. Bring to a boil. Reduce heat; cover and simmer for 8-12 minutes or until chicken is cooked through. Serve with rice; sprinkle with cheese.

Tuscan Chicken

I created this recipe one night when I was looking for a new way to prepare chicken. It's tender, saucy and healthy, too. I recently lost 30-some pounds, and this is one dish I prepared often.
—**CARLA WELLS** SOMERSET, KY

PREP: 25 MIN. • **COOK:** 15 MIN. • **MAKES:** 4 SERVINGS

- 4 boneless skinless chicken breast halves (6 ounces each)
- ¼ teaspoon pepper
- 2 tablespoons olive oil
- 1 each medium green, sweet red and yellow peppers, julienned
- 2 thin slices prosciutto or deli ham, chopped
- 2 garlic cloves, minced
- 1 can (14½ ounces) diced tomatoes, undrained
- ¼ cup reduced-sodium chicken broth
- 2 tablespoons minced fresh basil or 2 teaspoons dried basil
- 1 teaspoon minced fresh oregano or ¼ teaspoon dried oregano

1. Sprinkle chicken with pepper. In a large nonstick skillet, brown chicken in oil. Remove and keep warm. In the same skillet, saute peppers and prosciutto until peppers are tender. Add garlic; cook 1 minute longer.

2. Add the tomatoes, broth, basil, oregano and chicken. Bring to a boil. Reduce heat; cover and simmer for 12-15 minutes or until a meat thermometer reads 170°.

TUSCAN CHICKEN

CRUMB-COATED CHICKEN AND BLACKBERRY SALSA

SERVES 2

Crumb-Coated Chicken & Blackberry Salsa

Jalapeno-blackberry salsa sweetened with a touch of maple syrup is the best way to top this breaded chicken. It makes such a lovely dinner for 2, and in under 30 minutes.
—**TAMMY THOMAS** MORRISVILLE, VT

START TO FINISH: 25 MIN. • **MAKES:** 2 SERVINGS

- ½ cup fresh blackberries
- 1 jalapeno pepper, seeded and minced
- 2 tablespoons minced fresh cilantro
- 2 tablespoons chopped red onion
- 2 tablespoons maple syrup
- 2 tablespoons balsamic vinegar
- 2 boneless skinless chicken breast halves (5 ounces each)
- ⅛ teaspoon salt
- ⅛ teaspoon pepper
- ¼ cup all-purpose flour
- 1 egg, beaten
- ½ cup panko (Japanese) bread crumbs
- 1 tablespoon olive oil

1. In a small bowl, combine the first six ingredients. Cover and refrigerate until serving.

2. Flatten chicken to ¼-in. thickness; sprinkle with salt and pepper. Place the flour, egg and bread crumbs in separate shallow bowls. Coat chicken with flour, dip in egg, then coat with crumbs.

3. In a large skillet, cook chicken in oil over medium heat for 4-6 minutes on each side or until no longer pink. Serve with salsa.

NOTE *Wear disposable gloves when cutting hot peppers; the oils can burn skin. Avoid touching your face.*

Gnocchi Chicken Skillet

Potato gnocchi are little dumplings made from a dough of potatoes, flour and sometimes eggs. Look for gnocchi in the pasta, ethnic or frozen section of your grocery store.
—**TASTE OF HOME TEST KITCHEN**

START TO FINISH: 20 MIN.
MAKES: 4 SERVINGS

- 1 **package (16 ounces) potato gnocchi**
- 1 **pound ground chicken**
- ½ **cup chopped onion**
- 2 **tablespoons olive oil**
- 1 **jar (26 ounces) spaghetti sauce**
- ¼ **teaspoon salt**
- ¼ **to ½ teaspoon dried oregano**
  Shredded Parmesan cheese, optional

1. Cook gnocchi according to package directions. Meanwhile, in a large skillet, cook chicken and onion in oil over medium heat until chicken is no longer pink; drain if necessary. Stir in the spaghetti sauce, salt and oregano; cook for 5-10 minutes or until heated through.
2. Drain gnocchi; gently stir into skillet. Garnish servings with cheese if desired.

THAI CHICKEN
NOODLES

GNOCCHI CHICKEN
SKILLET

SERVES ②

Thai Chicken Noodles

I try to buy fresh chicken when it's on sale. I cook a big batch in the slow cooker, then shred it and package it in amounts suitable for recipes like this. When I want it, it just needs to be pulled out of the freezer and defrosted.
—**JENI PITTARD** COMMERCE, GA

START TO FINISH: 25 MIN.
MAKES: 2 SERVINGS

- 3 **ounces uncooked whole wheat linguine**
- ½ **cup salsa**
- 2 **tablespoons reduced-fat creamy peanut butter**
- 1 **tablespoon orange juice**
- 1½ **teaspoons honey**
- 1 **teaspoon reduced-sodium soy sauce**
- 1 **cup cubed cooked chicken breast**
- 1 **tablespoon chopped unsalted peanuts**
- 1 **tablespoon minced fresh cilantro**

1. Cook linguine according to package directions.

2. Meanwhile, in a microwave-safe dish, combine the salsa, peanut butter, orange juice, honey and soy sauce. Cover and microwave on high for 1 minute; stir. Add the chicken; heat through.
3. Drain linguine. Serve with chicken mixture. Garnish with peanuts and cilantro.
NOTE *This recipe was tested in a 1,100-watt microwave.*

Smooth Honey

Crystallization is the natural process by which liquid honey becomes solid. It's not uncommon for this to happen before you can use up the whole jar. To smooth it out, place honey in a microwave-safe container and heat on high, stirring every 30 seconds until the crystals dissolve.

SKILLET ZITI WITH CHICKEN AND BROCCOLI

Skillet Ziti with Chicken and Broccoli

I came across this recipe when I was looking for ways to use our bumper crop of red peppers. I've started roasting my own, but the jarred kind work well in this recipe.
—**TAMMY DIEKEMPER** MARINE, IL

START TO FINISH: 30 MIN.
MAKES: 4 SERVINGS

- 1 **pound boneless skinless chicken breasts, cut into ½-inch strips**
- ½ **teaspoon pepper**
- ¼ **teaspoon salt, divided**
- 2 **tablespoons butter, divided**
- 1 **small onion, chopped**
- 3 **garlic cloves, minced**
- ¼ **teaspoon crushed red pepper flakes**
- ¼ **teaspoon dried oregano**
- 2 **cups reduced-sodium chicken broth**
- 1 **cup fat-free milk**
- 2½ **cups uncooked ziti**
- 1 **bunch broccoli, cut into florets**
- 1 **cup julienned roasted sweet red peppers**
- ½ **cup grated Parmesan cheese**

1. Sprinkle chicken with pepper and ⅛ teaspoon salt. In a large skillet, saute chicken in 1 tablespoon butter until no longer pink. Remove and keep warm.

2. In the same skillet, saute onion in remaining butter until tender. Add the garlic, pepper flakes, oregano and remaining salt; cook 1 minute longer. Stir in broth and milk; bring to a boil. Add ziti; cook for 7-8 minutes or until ziti is tender, adding broccoli and red peppers during the last 5 minutes of cooking.

3. Return chicken to skillet; heat through. Sprinkle with cheese.

MEDITERRANEAN CHICKEN
WITH SPAGHETTI SQUASH

Mediterranean Chicken with Spaghetti Squash

Brimming with classic Mediterranean ingredients, this restaurant-quality dish will be an instant dinnertime hit. Serve it with a quick salad for a complete meal.

—JAYNE MARTIN STRATHCLAIR, MB

PREP: 35 MIN. • **COOK:** 35 MIN.
MAKES: 6 SERVINGS

- 1 medium spaghetti squash
- 1½ pounds boneless skinless chicken breasts, cut into ½-inch cubes
- 5 center-cut bacon strips, chopped
- 1 medium leek (white portion only), coarsely chopped
- 4 garlic cloves, minced
- 3 tablespoons all-purpose flour
- 1 cup reduced-sodium chicken broth
- ½ cup white wine or additional reduced-sodium chicken broth
- ⅓ cup half-and-half cream
- 2 plum tomatoes, chopped
- 1 can (2¼ ounces) sliced ripe olives, drained
- ⅓ cup grated Parmesan cheese
- 1½ teaspoons minced fresh sage or ½ teaspoon rubbed sage
- 1 teaspoon minced fresh thyme or ¼ teaspoon dried thyme
- ½ teaspoon salt
- ⅛ teaspoon pepper

1. Cut squash in half lengthwise; discard seeds. Place squash cut side down on a microwave-safe plate. Microwave, uncovered, on high for 15-18 minutes or until tender.
2. Meanwhile, in a large nonstick skillet coated with cooking spray, cook chicken over medium heat until no longer pink; drain. Remove from the skillet.
3. In the same skillet, cook bacon and leek over medium heat until bacon is crisp. Using a slotted spoon, remove bacon mixture to paper towels. Add garlic; cook for 1 minute. Stir in flour until blended; gradually add the broth, wine and cream. Bring to a boil; cook and stir for 1-2 minutes or until thickened. Stir in remaining ingredients. Add chicken and bacon mixture; heat through.
4. When squash is cool enough to handle, use a fork to separate strands. Serve with chicken mixture.

SERVES ②

Chicken Fricassee

This is one of our all-time favorite dinners. When you have guests over, just double the recipe.

—CAROL HEMKER PHENIX CITY, AL

PREP: 10 MIN. • **COOK:** 40 MIN.
MAKES: 2 SERVINGS

- 4½ teaspoons all-purpose flour, divided
- ¼ teaspoon salt
- ⅛ teaspoon pepper
- ⅛ teaspoon dried thyme
- 2 bone-in chicken thighs, skin removed (about ¾ pound)
- 2 tablespoons butter
- ¾ cup sliced fresh mushrooms
- ½ cup diced onion
- ¼ cup diced celery
- ¾ cup water
- 1 small bay leaf
- ¼ cup milk
- 2 teaspoons minced fresh parsley

1. In a resealable plastic bag, combine 2¼ teaspoons flour, salt, pepper and thyme. Add chicken and shake to coat. In a small skillet, brown chicken in butter. Remove chicken and set aside. In same skillet, saute mushrooms, onion and celery until crisp-tender. Return chicken to pan. Add water and bay leaf. Bring to a boil. Reduce heat; cover and simmer for 30-35 minutes or until chicken juices run clear, turning occasionally.
2. Place remaining flour in a bowl; stir in milk until smooth. Stir into pan juices. Bring to a boil; cook and stir for 2 minutes or until thickened. Discard bay leaf. Sprinkle with parsley.

Spicy Seasoned Chicken

For a quick and easy chicken fajita dinner, use this simple seasoning blend to spice things up. While you're at it, make a double batch of chicken and use the leftovers for taco salad.

—TASTE OF HOME TEST KITCHEN

START TO FINISH: 20 MIN.
MAKES: 4 SERVINGS

- 1 pound boneless skinless chicken breasts, cut into strips
- 1 teaspoon ground cumin
- 1 teaspoon garlic powder
- 1 teaspoon chili powder
- ½ teaspoon salt
- 1 tablespoon canola oil
- 4 flour tortillas (8 inches), warmed
  Shredded cheddar cheese, sliced ripe olives, shredded lettuce, sour cream and salsa, optional

In a large skillet, saute the chicken, cumin, garlic powder, chili powder and salt in oil until chicken is no longer pink. Serve with flour tortillas. Serve with toppings if desired.

SPICY SEASONED CHICKEN

I opened my pantry and found a box of mac & cheese mix. This is how I transformed it into a home-cooked dinner

—MARGARET WILSON SUN CITY, CA

Tuxedo Pasta

I try to keep leftover chicken or turkey on hand so I can fix this dish whenever I want. The wine sauce has a hint of lemon flavor that goes great with fresh basil.

—JACKIE HANNAHS BRETHREN, MI

START TO FINISH: 20 MIN.
MAKES: 6 SERVINGS

- 2 cups uncooked bow tie pasta
- 2 cups cubed cooked chicken
- 1 medium zucchini, sliced
- 1½ cups sliced fresh mushrooms
- ½ cup chopped sweet red pepper
- 3 tablespoons butter, divided
- ¼ cup lemon juice
- 2 tablespoons white wine or chicken broth
- ¾ cup shredded Parmesan cheese
- 3 tablespoons minced fresh basil or 1 tablespoon dried basil

1. Cook pasta according to package directions. Meanwhile, in a large skillet, saute the chicken, zucchini, mushrooms and red pepper in 2 tablespoons butter for 4-5 minutes or until vegetables are tender. Add the lemon juice and wine. Bring to a boil. Reduce heat; cook and stir for 2 minutes or until heated through.
2. Drain pasta; add to skillet. Stir in the cheese, basil and remaining butter.

MAC AND CHEESE CHICKEN SKILLET

Mac and Cheese Chicken Skillet

START TO FINISH: 30 MIN.
MAKES: 6 SERVINGS

- 1 pound boneless skinless chicken breasts, cut into 1-inch cubes
- 1 teaspoon olive oil
- 1 package (7¼ ounces) macaroni and cheese dinner mix
- 2½ cups chicken broth
- 1 cup chopped zucchini
- ½ cup chopped onion
- 1 teaspoon dried oregano
- 1 can (14½ ounces) Italian stewed tomatoes, drained

1. In a large skillet, cook chicken in oil over medium-high heat until no longer pink.
2. Set aside the cheese packet from the macaroni dinner mix. Stir in the pasta, broth, zucchini, onion and oregano. Bring to a boil. Reduce heat; cover and simmer for 7-8 minutes or until pasta is tender, stirring occasionally.
3. Stir in tomatoes and the contents of the reserved cheese packet. Cook and stir for 3-4 minutes or until heated through.

TUXEDO PASTA

Olive 'n' Fig Chicken

I love green olives and figs, so I put them together with chicken for a salty-sweet combination that's perfect for a special meal.
—CAROL HULL HERMISTON, OR

START TO FINISH: 25 MIN. • **MAKES:** 4 SERVINGS

- 4 boneless skinless chicken breast halves (5 ounces each)
- ¼ teaspoon garlic salt
- ¼ teaspoon lemon-pepper seasoning
- 2 tablespoons olive oil
- 1 jar (6.35 ounces) green olive tapenade
- 2 tablespoons fig preserves
  Sliced pimiento-stuffed olives, optional

1. Flatten chicken to ½-inch thickness; sprinkle with garlic salt and lemon-pepper. In a large skillet, cook chicken in oil over medium heat for 4-5 minutes on each side or until a thermometer reads 170°. Remove and keep warm.
2. In the same skillet, cook tapenade and fig preserves over medium heat until heated through, stirring to loosen browned bits from pan. Return chicken to the pan; cook on low heat for 2-3 minutes or until chicken is heated through. Garnish with olives if desired.

TROPICAL MANDARIN CHICKEN

Blackened Chicken and Beans

My husband loves any spicy food, and this is one quick-fix and low-fat recipe we can both agree on. As the chicken cooks, I whip up salads with lettuce, tomato, avocado and shredded cheddar cheese. Dinner's done!
—CHRISTINE ZONGKER SPRING HILL, KS

START TO FINISH: 20 MIN. • **MAKES:** 4 SERVINGS

- 2 teaspoons chili powder
- ¼ teaspoon salt
- ¼ teaspoon pepper
- 4 boneless skinless chicken breast halves (4 ounces each)
- 1 tablespoon canola oil
- 1 can (15 ounces) black beans, rinsed and drained
- 1 cup frozen corn
- 1 cup chunky salsa

1. Combine the chili powder, salt and pepper; rub over both sides of chicken. In a large nonstick skillet, cook chicken in oil over medium heat for 4-5 minutes on each side or until a thermometer reads 170°. Remove and keep warm.
2. Add the beans, corn and salsa to the pan; heat through. Serve with chicken.

Tropical Mandarin Chicken

This tropical medley was a favorite of my mother-in-law. She's since passed away, but I love to make it for my father-in-law because it was their special dish.
—LYNDA HEMINGER YANKTON, SD

START TO FINISH: 30 MIN. • **MAKES:** 6 SERVINGS

- 6 boneless skinless chicken breast halves (6 ounces each)
- 1 tablespoon olive oil
- 2 tablespoons all-purpose flour
- ½ cup chicken broth
- 1½ cups orange juice
- 1 medium green pepper, chopped
- 1 medium sweet red pepper, chopped
- 1 can (11 ounces) mandarin oranges, drained
- 1 cup pineapple chunks
- ⅓ cup golden raisins
- ⅛ to ¼ teaspoon crushed red pepper flakes
- ⅛ teaspoon salt
- ⅛ teaspoon pepper
  Hot cooked rice, optional

1. Flatten chicken to ½-in. thickness. In a large skillet, cook chicken in oil for 4-5 minutes on each side or until no longer pink. Remove chicken and keep warm.
2. In a small bowl, combine flour and broth until smooth; stir into skillet. Add the orange juice, peppers, oranges, pineapple, raisins, pepper flakes, salt and pepper. Bring to a boil; cook and stir for 2 minutes or until thickened. Return chicken to the pan; heat through. Serve with rice if desired.

Stovetop Chicken 'n' Stuffing

With nothing in mind for dinner, I just started messing around and voila, this meal-in-one was created. My family was quite happy with it.
—**CONNIE JONAS** EUGENE, OR

START TO FINISH: 30 MIN. • **MAKES:** 4 SERVINGS

- 1 **package (6 ounces) corn bread stuffing mix**
- ½ **cup all-purpose flour**
- 1 **teaspoon salt**
- 1 **teaspoon ground mustard**
- 4 **boneless skinless chicken breast halves (6 ounces each)**
- 1 **tablespoon canola oil**
- 1 **can (10¾ ounces) condensed cream of mushroom soup, undiluted**
- ⅔ **cup chopped onion**
- ⅔ **cup milk**
- 2 **tablespoons crumbled cooked bacon**
- 2 **cans (14½ ounces each) cut green beans, drained**
- ½ **cup shredded Monterey Jack cheese**

1. Prepare stuffing mix according to package directions. Meanwhile, in a large resealable plastic bag, combine the flour, salt and mustard. Add chicken, a few pieces at a time, and shake to coat.
2. In a large skillet, cook chicken in oil for 2-3 minutes on each side or until golden brown.
3. In a large bowl, combine the soup, onion, milk and bacon; stir in green beans. Pour over chicken; top with stuffing. Cover and cook for 7 minutes.
4. Sprinkle with cheese; cook 3-4 minutes longer or until heated through and cheese is melted.

Mediterranean Chicken & Beans

Not only does this cooking method make really juicy chicken thighs, it saves you time scrubbing an extra pan.
—**MARIE RIZZIO** INTERLOCHEN, MI

PREP: 25 MIN. • **COOK:** 20 MIN. • **MAKES:** 6 SERVINGS

- 2 **tablespoons all-purpose flour**
- 1 **teaspoon garlic salt**
- 1 **teaspoon dried rosemary, crushed**
- ½ **teaspoon pepper**
- 6 **bone-in chicken thighs (about 2¼ pounds), skin removed**
- 2 **tablespoons olive oil**
- 1 **can (15 ounces) white kidney or cannellini beans, rinsed and drained**
- 1 **can (14½ ounces) diced tomatoes, undrained**
- 6 **slices provolone cheese**

1. In a large resealable plastic bag, combine the flour, garlic salt, rosemary and pepper. Add chicken, a few pieces at a time, and shake to coat.
2. In a large skillet, brown chicken in oil. Stir in beans and tomatoes; bring to a boil. Reduce heat. Cover and simmer for 20-25 minutes or until chicken juices run clear. Remove from the heat. Top with cheese. Cover and let stand for 5 minutes or until cheese is melted.

STOVETOP CHICKEN 'N' STUFFING

MAKEOVER BACON
CHICKEN ALFREDO

Makeover Bacon Chicken Alfredo

This healthier version of bacon chicken Alfredo offers all the creamy comfort and rich homey flavor of the original, but slashes the calories, cholesterol and sodium content.

—**IRENE SULLIVAN** LAKE MILLS, WI

PREP: 30 MIN. • **COOK:** 15 MIN.
MAKES: 8 SERVINGS

- 1 package (16 ounces) whole wheat fettuccine
- 8 bacon strips, chopped
- 1 pound boneless skinless chicken breasts, cubed
- ½ teaspoon salt, divided
- ¼ teaspoon pepper
- 2 garlic cloves, minced
- 1 tablespoon butter
- 3 tablespoons cornstarch
- 3 cups 2% milk
- 1 cup half-and-half cream
- 1 package (10 ounces) frozen chopped spinach, thawed and squeezed dry
- 1 cup grated Parmigiano-Reggiano cheese, divided
- ½ teaspoon Italian seasoning

1. Cook fettuccine according to package directions. Meanwhile, in a large skillet, cook bacon over medium heat until crisp. Remove to paper towels to drain.
2. Sprinkle chicken with ¼ teaspoon salt and pepper. Cook chicken and garlic in butter over medium heat for 4-6 minutes or until meat is no longer pink; remove and keep warm.
3. Combine cornstarch and milk until smooth; stir into skillet. Add cream and remaining salt. Bring to a boil; cook and stir for 2 minutes or until thickened. Add the spinach, chicken, ¾ cup cheese, Italian seasoning and half of the bacon; cook and stir until cheese is melted.
4. Drain fettuccine; add to chicken mixture. Cook and stir until heated through. Sprinkle with remaining cheese and bacon.

Creamy Chicken Tortellini

I'm always trying to come up with new recipes. For this one, I just started combining ingredients. The result was so rich and creamy, I knew it was a keeper.

—**TIFFANY TREANOR** WAUKOMIS, OK

START TO FINISH: 30 MIN.
MAKES: 3 SERVINGS

- 1½ cups frozen cheese tortellini
- 1 boneless skinless chicken breast half (6 ounces), cut into 1-inch cubes
- 3 bacon strips, chopped
- ⅛ teaspoon adobo seasoning
- ⅓ cup chopped onion
- ⅓ cup chopped sweet red pepper
- 3 teaspoons minced garlic
- 1 can (10¾ ounces) condensed cream of chicken soup, undiluted
- ½ cup 2% milk
- ⅓ cup sour cream
- 2 tablespoons grated Parmesan cheese
- 1 cup frozen chopped broccoli, thawed and drained

1. Cook tortellini according to package directions. Meanwhile, in a large saucepan, cook and stir the chicken, bacon and adobo seasoning over medium heat until chicken is no longer pink. Add onion and red pepper; cook and stir until tender. Add garlic; cook 1 minute longer.
2. In a small bowl, combine the soup, milk, sour cream and cheese; stir into chicken mixture. Bring to a boil. Reduce heat; simmer, uncovered, for 5-7 minutes.
3. Drain tortellini; add to chicken mixture. Stir in broccoli; heat through.

CREAMY CHICKEN TORTELLINI

SMOTHERED
HOME-STYLE CHICKEN

Summertime Orzo & Chicken

For lunch or dinner, this easy-as-can-be dish is likely to become a summer staple in your house. It's that good.

—FRAN MACMILLAN WEST MELBOURNE, FL

START TO FINISH: 30 MIN.
MAKES: 4 SERVINGS

- ¾ cup uncooked orzo pasta
- 1 pound boneless skinless chicken breasts, cut into 1-inch pieces
- 1 medium cucumber, chopped
- 1 small red onion, chopped
- ¼ cup minced fresh parsley
- 2 tablespoons lemon juice
- 1 tablespoon olive oil
- 1 teaspoon salt
- ¼ teaspoon pepper
- ¼ cup crumbled reduced-fat feta cheese

1. Cook pasta according to package directions. Meanwhile, in a large skillet coated with cooking spray, cook chicken over medium heat for 6-8 minutes or until no longer pink.
2. In a large bowl, combine the cucumber, onion, parsley and chicken. Drain pasta; stir into chicken mixture. In a small bowl, whisk the lemon juice, oil, salt and pepper. Pour over chicken mixture; toss to coat. Serve warm or cold. Just before serving, sprinkle with cheese.

SUMMERTIME ORZO & CHICKEN

Cajun Country Fried Chicken

I like to make my own cajun seasonings using a blend of herbs and spices, but in this recipe a store-bought variety works just as well.

—DAVE FISHER TEN MILE, TN

PREP: 15 MIN. + MARINATING
COOK: 10 MIN.
MAKES: 8-10 SERVINGS

- 2 cups milk
- 2 tablespoons Cajun seasoning, divided
- 8 boneless skinless chicken breast halves
- 4 boneless skinless chicken thighs (about 1 pound), halved
- 1¼ cups all-purpose flour
- ½ teaspoon lemon-pepper seasoning
- ½ teaspoon garlic salt
  Oil for frying

1. In a large bowl, combine milk and 1 tablespoon Cajun seasoning; add chicken. Cover and refrigerate for at least 2 hours.
2. In a large resealable plastic bag, combine the flour, lemon-pepper, garlic salt and remaining Cajun seasoning. Drain chicken and discard milk mixture. Place chicken in flour mixture and shake to coat.
3. In a skillet, heat ¼ in. of oil; fry chicken for 7-8 minutes or until juices run clear.

Smothered Home-Style Chicken

I serve this creamy chicken with rice and use the broth as gravy over each. You can add a slurry of corn starch and water to thicken the sauce, but I don't think it's necessary.

—BILLY HENSLEY MOUNT CARMEL, TN

START TO FINISH: 30 MIN.
MAKES: 5 SERVINGS

- ⅓ cup all-purpose flour
- 1 teaspoon salt
- 1 teaspoon garlic powder
- 1 teaspoon Cajun seasoning
- 1 teaspoon pepper
- 5 boneless skinless chicken thighs (about 1½ pounds)
- 3 tablespoons olive oil, divided
- 2 medium carrots, chopped
- 1 small onion, chopped
- ½ cup chopped green pepper
- 2 garlic cloves, minced
- ½ cup white wine or chicken broth
- 1 can (10¾ ounces) condensed cream of chicken soup, undiluted
- ½ cup chicken broth
  Hot cooked rice

1. In a large resealable plastic bag, combine flour, salt, garlic powder, Cajun seasoning and pepper. Add chicken thighs, one at a time, and shake to coat. In a large skillet, brown chicken in 2 tablespoons oil in batches. Remove and keep warm.
2. In same skillet, saute carrots, onion and green pepper in remaining oil until tender. Add garlic; cook 1 minute. Add wine, stirring to loosen browned bits from pan. Stir in soup and broth.
3. Return chicken to skillet. Bring to a boil. Reduce heat; cover and simmer for 10-15 minutes or until a thermometer reads 165°. Serve with rice.

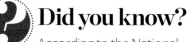

Did you know?

According to the National Chicken Council, more than 1.25 billion chicken wing portions were consumed on Super Bowl weekend in 2012. That's more than 100 million pounds of chicken!

Creamy Chicken and Pasta

Rich, creamy and laced with wine, this homemade sauce is one my family loves. Use it over pasta and chicken for a dinner you'll be proud to serve. I also add capers to lend a salty, lemony flavor to pasta.
—ELAINE MOSER SPOKANE, WA

START TO FINISH: 30 MIN.
MAKES: 5 SERVINGS

- 2 cups uncooked penne pasta
- 2 cups sliced fresh mushrooms
- 1 cup sliced green onions
- 2 tablespoons butter
- ½ cup white wine or chicken broth
- 1 teaspoon minced garlic
- 1 tablespoon all-purpose flour
- ⅓ cup water
- 1 cup heavy whipping cream
- 2 cups cubed cooked chicken
- 2 tablespoons capers, drained
- ¼ teaspoon salt
- ⅛ teaspoon pepper
  Shredded Parmesan cheese

1. Cook pasta according to package directions. Meanwhile, in a large skillet, saute mushrooms and onions in butter for 4-5 minutes or until tender. Add wine or broth and garlic. Bring to a boil; cook until liquid is reduced by half, about 5 minutes.

2. Combine flour and water until smooth; gradually add to mushroom mixture. Bring to a boil. Reduce heat; cook and stir for 2 minutes or until thickened. Stir in cream. Bring to a boil. Reduce heat; simmer, uncovered, for 4-5 minutes or until heated through.

3. Drain pasta. Add the pasta, chicken, capers, salt and pepper to cream sauce. Cook for 3-4 minutes or until heated through. Sprinkle with Parmesan cheese.

Cranberry-Orange Chicken

My husband and I have a small bog. So I experiment with cranberry recipes every fall. I came across this one in a cookbook, then just changed around a few things to better suit our tastes.
—SHARON PARSONS KILLINGWORTH, CT

PREP: 25 MIN. • **COOK:** 1 HOUR
MAKES: 4-6 SERVINGS

- ½ cup all-purpose flour
- ⅛ teaspoon salt
- 1 broiler/fryer chicken (about 3 pounds), cut up
- 4 tablespoons butter
- 2 cups whole fresh or frozen cranberries
- ½ cup chopped onion
- 2 tablespoons grated orange peel
- 1¼ cups sugar
- 1¼ cups orange juice
- ¼ teaspoon ground ginger
- ¼ teaspoon ground cinnamon
  Red food coloring, optional

1. Combine the flour and salt and place in a plastic bag. Shake chicken, a few pieces at a time, in flour mixture. Melt butter in a large skillet; brown chicken on all sides.

2. In a saucepan, combine remaining ingredients except food coloring; bring to a boil. Pour over chicken; cover and simmer for 1 hour or until a thermometer reads 180°. Remove chicken to a warm platter.

3. Bring sauce to a boil and cook, stirring frequently, until thickened. Add a few drops red food coloring if desired. Serve with chicken.

LEMONY SPINACH-STUFFED CHICKEN BREASTS

Lemony Spinach-Stuffed Chicken Breasts

Caramelizing the onions first adds a world of flavor to the filling for this chicken. I usually serve this dish with couscous, rice or garlic mashed potatoes along with a vegetable saute or tossed salad.
—PAM NELSON BEAVERTON, OR

PREP: 30 MIN. • **COOK:** 20 MIN.
MAKES: 4 SERVINGS

- ½ cup chopped sweet onion
- 3 teaspoons olive oil, divided
- 6½ cups fresh baby spinach, chopped
- 1 garlic clove, minced
- 1 tablespoon balsamic vinegar
- ¼ cup crumbled feta cheese
- ½ teaspoon grated lemon peel
- ¼ teaspoon salt
- ¼ teaspoon pepper
- 4 boneless skinless chicken breast halves (6 ounces each)

1. In a large skillet, cook onion in 2 teaspoons oil over medium heat for 15-20 minutes or until onion is golden brown, stirring frequently. Add the spinach, garlic and vinegar; cook 1 minute longer. Remove from the heat; cool for 5 minutes. Stir in the cheese, lemon peel, salt and pepper.

2. Flatten chicken to ¼-in. thickness. Spread spinach mixture over chicken. Roll up and secure with toothpicks.

3. In a large skillet over medium heat, cook chicken in remaining oil for 8-10 minutes on each side or until chicken juices run clear. Discard toothpicks.

CREAMY CHICKEN AND PASTA

Applesauce Barbecue Chicken

START TO FINISH: 20 MIN. • **MAKES:** 4 SERVINGS

- 4 boneless skinless chicken breast halves (6 ounces each)
- ½ teaspoon pepper
- 1 tablespoon olive oil
- ⅔ cup chunky applesauce
- ⅔ cup spicy barbecue sauce
- 2 tablespoons brown sugar
- 1 teaspoon chili powder

Sprinkle chicken with pepper. In a large skillet, brown chicken in oil on both sides. In a small bowl, combine the remaining ingredients; pour over chicken. Cover and cook 7-10 minutes longer or until a meat thermometer reads 170°.

You only need a few ingredients to create sweet and peppery chicken. The subtle flavor of apple sets this dish apart from the rest.

—DARLA ANDREWS LEWISVILLE, TX

APPLESAUCE BARBECUE CHICKEN

CHICKEN MARSALA WITH GORGONZOLA

Chicken Marsala with Gorgonzola

Chicken topped with melted Gorgonzola is quick enough for weeknight cooking but also elegant enough for a dinner party. We live near the Faribault, MN, caves that are used to age the lovely Amableu Gorgonzola cheese, so this is a favorite for us.

—JILL ANDERSON SLEEPY EYE, MN

PREP: 10 MIN. • **COOK:** 30 MIN. • **MAKES:** 4 SERVINGS

- 4 boneless skinless chicken breast halves (6 ounces each)
- ¼ teaspoon plus ⅛ teaspoon salt, divided
- ¼ teaspoon pepper
- 3 tablespoons olive oil, divided
- ½ pound sliced baby portobello mushrooms
- 2 garlic cloves, minced
- 1 cup Marsala wine
- ⅔ cup heavy whipping cream
- ½ cup crumbled Gorgonzola cheese, divided
- 2 tablespoons minced fresh parsley

1. Sprinkle chicken with ¼ teaspoon salt and pepper. In a large skillet, cook chicken in 2 tablespoons oil over medium heat 6-8 minutes on each side or until a thermometer reads 165°. Remove and keep warm.

2. In same skillet, saute mushrooms in remaining oil until tender. Add garlic; cook 1 minute.

3. Add wine, stirring to loosen browned bits from pan. Bring to a boil; cook until liquid is reduced by a third. Stir in cream and remaining salt. Return to a boil; cook until slightly thickened.

4. Return chicken to pan; add ⅓ cup cheese. Cook until cheese is melted. Sprinkle with remaining cheese; garnish with parsley.

Peach Chicken

This fruity and savory entree will appeal to the whole family. The chicken's bread crumb coating makes it especially homey.

—TASTE OF HOME TEST KITCHEN

START TO FINISH: 30 MIN. • **MAKES:** 4 SERVINGS

- 1 can (15 ounces) sliced peaches in extra-light syrup
- 2 teaspoons cornstarch
- ¼ cup peach preserves
- 1 tablespoon white wine or chicken broth
- ¼ cup seasoned bread crumbs
- 1 tablespoon grated Parmesan cheese
- ¼ teaspoon salt
- ¼ teaspoon pepper
- 4 boneless skinless chicken breast halves (6 ounces each)
- 2 tablespoons butter, divided
- 2 green onions, chopped
  Hot cooked pasta

1. Drain peaches, reserving juice. In a small bowl, combine cornstarch and reserved juice until smooth. Add preserves and wine; set aside.

2. In a large resealable plastic bag, combine the bread crumbs, cheese, salt and pepper. Add chicken, one piece at a time, and shake to coat. In a large skillet, cook chicken in 1 tablespoon butter over medium heat for 4-6 minutes on each side or until chicken juices run clear. Remove and keep warm.

3. In the same skillet, melt remaining butter. Stir cornstarch mixture and add to pan. Bring to a boil; cook and stir for 2 minutes or until thickened. Add chicken and peaches; heat through. Sprinkle with onions; serve with pasta.

SOLO CHICKEN STROGANOFF

SERVES ①

Solo Chicken Stroganoff

I use chicken breasts as a base for building a variety of meals. This quick meal requires only one skillet plus a pan for the rice or pasta. Sometimes I change the recipe by adding a half cup of uncooked rice after the chicken and veggies have been sauteed.

—BILL HILBRICH ST. CLOUD, MN

START TO FINISH: 25 MIN. • **MAKES:** 1 SERVING.

- 1 boneless skinless chicken breast half, cut into 2-inch strips
- 1 cup sliced fresh mushrooms
- ⅓ cup chopped onion
- ⅓ cup chopped green pepper
- 2 tablespoons butter
- 2 tablespoons all-purpose flour
- ½ cup chicken broth
- 2 tablespoons sour cream
- ¼ teaspoon salt
- ⅛ to ¼ teaspoon pepper
- ⅛ teaspoon ground nutmeg
  Hot cooked pasta

1. In a large skillet, saute the chicken, mushrooms, onion and green pepper in butter until chicken is no longer pink. Combine flour and broth until smooth; gradually add to the skillet. Bring to a boil; cook and stir for 2 minutes or until thickened.

2. Reduce heat. Add the sour cream, salt, pepper and nutmeg; cook and stir until heated through (do not boil). Serve over pasta.

PEACH CHICKEN

Corn Bread Chicken Tenders

These golden tenders are cooked in only a small amount of oil, so there's very little fat. The chicken is crisp and ready to eat in about 6 minutes.

—**ANGELA BOTTGER** NEW CANAAN, CT

START TO FINISH: 15 MIN.
MAKES: 2 SERVINGS

- ¼ cup corn bread/muffin mix
- 3 tablespoons prepared ranch salad dressing
- 6 chicken tenderloins
- 2 teaspoons canola oil

1. Place corn bread mix and salad dressing in separate shallow bowls. Dip chicken in dressing, then roll in corn bread mix.
2. In a large skillet, cook chicken in oil over medium heat for 3-4 minutes on each side or until meat is no longer pink.

Savory Onion Chicken

Soup mix and beer go a long way to flavor this chicken. Use a style of beer you like; the taste comes through more than you would expect, and the leftover beer gravy would go great over mashed potatoes.

—**JULIA ANDERSON** RINGGOLD, GA

START TO FINISH: 30 MIN.
MAKES: 6 SERVINGS

- ¼ cup all-purpose flour, divided
- 1 broiler/fryer chicken (3 to 4 pounds), cut up and skin removed
- 2 tablespoons olive oil
- 1 envelope onion soup mix
- 1 bottle (12 ounces) beer or nonalcoholic beer

1. Place 2 tablespoons flour in a large resealable plastic bag. Add chicken, a few pieces at a time, and shake to coat. In a large skillet, brown chicken in oil on all sides. Remove and keep warm.

2. Add soup mix and remaining flour, stirring to loosen browned bits from pan. Gradually whisk in beer. Bring to a boil; cook and stir for 2 minutes or until thickened.
3. Return chicken to the pan. Bring to a boil. Reduce heat; cover and simmer for 12-15 minutes or until chicken juices run clear.

Chicken with Tomato-Cream Sauce

Sour cream gives this tomato sauce extra body and richness. Because this recipe is so easy to double, it's great for entertaining a crowd.

—**AGNES COOPER** NEWARK, DE

PREP: 5 MIN. • **COOK:** 40 MIN.
MAKES: 8 SERVINGS

- 8 boneless skinless chicken breast halves
- ¼ cup butter
- 1 small onion, thinly sliced
- 2 garlic cloves, minced
- 1 can (14½ ounces) diced tomatoes, undrained
- 1 teaspoon salt
- 2 tablespoons all-purpose flour
- 1 cup (8 ounces) sour cream
- ⅔ cup grated Parmesan cheese
  Hot cooked noodles

1. In a large skillet, brown chicken in butter on each side. Remove and set aside. Add onion and garlic; saute until tender. Stir in tomatoes and salt. Bring to a boil. Reduce heat; return chicken to pan. Cover and simmer for 30 minutes or until chicken juices run clear.
2. Remove chicken and keep warm. Combine the flour and sour cream. Reduce heat to low; stir in sour cream mixture and Parmesan cheese. Heat through (do not boil). Serve chicken and sauce over noodles.

CORN BREAD CHICKEN TENDERS

 **Did you know?**

When families dine together, they tend to eat more vegetables and fruits and fewer fried foods.

SHREDDED BARBECUE
CHICKEN OVER GRITS

Shredded Barbecue Chicken over Grits

It's an unusual combination with pumpkin and pepper jack cheese but the flavor is fantastic. The grits thicken up nicely, and the sweet, smoky barbecue chicken practically melts in your mouth.

—**ERIN RENOUF MYLROIE** SANTA CLARA, UT

PREP: 20 MIN. • **COOK:** 25 MIN.
MAKES: 6 SERVINGS

- 1 **pound boneless skinless chicken breasts**
- ¼ **teaspoon pepper**
- 1 **can (14½ ounces) reduced-sodium chicken broth, divided**
- 1 **cup hickory smoke-flavored barbecue sauce**
- ¼ **cup molasses**
- 1 **tablespoon ground ancho chili pepper**
- ½ **teaspoon ground cinnamon**
- 2¼ **cups water**
- 1 **cup quick-cooking grits**
- 1 **cup canned pumpkin**
- ¾ **cup shredded pepper Jack cheese**
- 1 **medium tomato, seeded and chopped**
- 6 **tablespoons reduced-fat sour cream**
- 2 **green onions, chopped**
- 2 **tablespoons minced fresh cilantro**

1. Sprinkle chicken with pepper; place in a large nonstick skillet coated with cooking spray.
2. In a large bowl, combine 1 cup broth, barbecue sauce, molasses, chili pepper and cinnamon; pour over chicken. Bring to a boil. Reduce heat; cover and simmer for 20-25 minutes or until a meat thermometer reads 170°. Shred meat with two forks and return to the skillet.
3. Meanwhile, in a large saucepan, bring water and remaining broth to a boil. Slowly stir in grits and pumpkin. Reduce heat; cook and stir for 5-7 minutes or until thickened. Stir in cheese until melted.
4. Divide grits among six serving bowls; top each with ½ cup chicken mixture. Serve with tomato, sour cream, green onions and cilantro.

Chicken and Sausage Penne

Gather the clan for a comfy-cozy dinner filled with two types of meat and a garlic-cream sauce. Sub in whatever cream soup and cheese you have on hand.

—**SANDRA PERRIN** NEW IBERIA, LA

START TO FINISH: 30 MIN.
MAKES: 8 SERVINGS

- 1 **package (16 ounces) penne pasta**
- 1 **pound boneless skinless chicken breasts, cubed**
- ¾ **pound smoked Polish sausage or fully cooked bratwurst links, cubed**
- 1 **medium onion, chopped**
- 1 **medium sweet red pepper, chopped**
- 1 **medium green pepper, chopped**
- 2 **tablespoons olive oil**
- 6 **garlic cloves, minced**
- 2 **jars (16 ounces each) Parmesan Alfredo sauce**
- 1 **can (10¾ ounces) condensed cream of mushroom soup, undiluted**
- ½ **teaspoon pepper**
- ¼ **teaspoon salt**
- 2 **cups (8 ounces) shredded cheddar cheese**

1. Cook pasta according to package directions. Meanwhile, in a Dutch oven, cook the chicken, sausage, onion and red and green peppers in oil over medium heat for 6-8 minutes or until chicken is no longer pink. Add garlic; cook and stir 1 minute longer.
2. Stir in the Alfredo sauce, soup, pepper and salt. Bring to boil. Reduce heat; simmer, uncovered, for 2 minutes. Stir in cheese. Drain pasta; add to chicken mixture and toss to coat.
3. Serve desired amount immediately. Cool remaining mixture; transfer to freezer containers. Freeze for up to 3 months.
TO USE FROZEN PASTA *Thaw in the refrigerator overnight. Transfer to a large skillet; cook and stir over medium heat for 10-12 minutes or until heated through.*
TO MICROWAVE FROZEN PASTA *Thaw in the refrigerator overnight. Transfer to a microwave-safe dish. Cover and microwave on high for 10-12 minutes or until heated through, stirring once.*

CHICKEN AND SAUSAGE
PENNE

**LEMON AND SAGE
ROASTED CHICKEN**
PAGE 71

Casseroles & Oven Entrees

{ **TEXAN RANCH CHICKEN CASSEROLE** *PAGE 64* }

{ **CREAMY CHICKEN ENCHILADAS** *PAGE 74* }

{ **BACON-CHEESE TOPPED CHICKEN** *PAGE 85* }

SERVES 2

Chicken Macaroni Casserole

Start the evening off right with this piping hot, comforting casserole for two. Topped with crispy bread crumbs, it has a satisfying crunch.

—**QUINCIE BALL** SHELTON, WA

PREP: 20 MIN. • **BAKE:** 20 MIN. • **MAKES:** 2 SERVINGS

- ⅔ **cup uncooked elbow macaroni**
- ⅔ **cup sliced fresh mushrooms**
- 2 **tablespoons finely chopped onion**
- 1 **tablespoon finely chopped green pepper**
- 1 **tablespoon butter**
- ¾ **cup cubed cooked chicken**
- ½ **cup shredded cheddar cheese**
- ½ **cup sour cream**
- 2 **tablespoons 2% milk**
- 1 **tablespoon chopped pimiento-stuffed olives**
- ½ **teaspoon seasoned salt**
- ⅛ **teaspoon pepper**
- ¼ **cup soft bread crumbs**
- 1 **teaspoon butter, melted**

1. Cook macaroni according to package directions. Meanwhile, in a small skillet, saute the mushrooms, onion and green pepper in butter until tender.
2. In a small bowl, combine the chicken, cheese, sour cream, milk, olives, seasoned salt, pepper and vegetable mixture. Drain macaroni; add to chicken mixture.
3. Transfer to a 3-cup baking dish coated with cooking spray. Combine bread crumbs and butter; sprinkle over top of casserole. Bake, uncovered, at 350° for 20-25 minutes or until bubbly.

CHICKEN MACARONI CASSEROLE

BAKED CHICKEN CHIMICHANGAS

Baked Chicken Chimichangas

I developed this quick and easy recipe through trial and error. I used to garnish it with sour cream, too, but eliminated it in order to lighten the recipe. My friends all love it when I cook these, and they're much healthier than deep-fried chimichangas.

—**RICKEY MADDEN** CLINTON, SC

PREP: 20 MIN. • **BAKE:** 20 MIN. • **MAKES:** 6 SERVINGS

- 1½ **cups cubed cooked chicken breast**
- 1½ **cups picante sauce, divided**
- ½ **cup shredded reduced-fat cheddar cheese**
- ⅔ **cup chopped green onions, divided**
- 1 **teaspoon ground cumin**
- 1 **teaspoon dried oregano**
- 6 **flour tortillas (8 inches), warmed**
- 1 **tablespoon butter, melted**

1. In a small bowl, combine the chicken, ¾ cup picante sauce, cheese, ¼ cup onions, cumin and oregano. Spoon ½ cup mixture down the center of each tortilla. Fold sides and ends over filling and roll up. Place seam side down in a 15-in. x 10-in. x 1-in. baking pan coated with cooking spray. Brush with butter.
2. Bake, uncovered, at 375° for 20-25 minutes or until heated through. Top with remaining sauce and onions.
Freeze Option *Before baking, cover and freeze casserole for up to 3 months. To use frozen casserole: Thaw in refrigerator overnight. Remove from refrigerator 30 minutes before baking. Bake according to directions.*

Smoked Gouda Spinach Pizza

A refrigerated pizza crust and store-bought Alfredo sauce make this pizza easy. My daughter created it as an appetizer, but we often have it for a main course. And the leftovers pack beautifully for a workday lunch.

—MARIE HATTRUP SPARKS, NV

START TO FINISH: 30 MIN. • **MAKES:** 10 PIECES

- 1 tube (13.8 ounces) refrigerated pizza crust
- ½ pound sliced fresh mushrooms
- 1 small red onion, chopped
- 2 tablespoons butter
- 2 garlic cloves, minced
- 1 cup Alfredo sauce
- ½ teaspoon dried thyme
- 1 package (6 ounces) fresh baby spinach
- ½ pound fully cooked Italian chicken sausage links, sliced
- 2 cups (8 ounces) shredded smoked Gouda cheese

1. Unroll dough into a greased 15-in. x 10-in. x 1-in. baking pan; flatten dough and build up edges slightly. Bake at 425° for 10-12 minutes or until lightly browned.

2. Meanwhile, saute mushrooms and onion in butter in a large skillet until tender. Add garlic; cook 1 minute longer. Stir in Alfredo sauce and thyme. Spread over crust. Top with spinach, sausage and cheese.

3. Bake for 10-15 minutes or until crust and cheese are lightly browned.

SMOKED GOUDA SPINACH PIZZA

CHEESY CHICKEN 'N' SHELLS

Cheesy Chicken 'n' Shells

When our friend served us this entree, I asked her for the recipe right away. It is so good, I thought I would share it with others. I cut the recipe down to serve just a few, but it can easily be doubled or tripled.

—JODEE HARDING MOUNT VERNON, OH

PREP: 15 MIN. • **BAKE:** 30 MIN. • **MAKES:** 2-4 SERVINGS

- 1½ cups uncooked medium shell pasta
- 2 tablespoons all-purpose flour
- ¼ cup water
- 1¼ cups chicken broth
- 1 can (10¾ ounces) condensed cream of chicken soup, undiluted
- ½ cup diced process cheese (Velveeta)
- ¼ teaspoon salt
- ¼ teaspoon pepper
- ¼ teaspoon poultry seasoning
- ⅛ teaspoon paprika
- 1½ cups cubed cooked chicken
- 3 tablespoons dry bread crumbs
- 1 tablespoon butter, melted

1. Preheat oven to 350°. Cook pasta according to package directions.

2. Meanwhile, in a saucepan, combine the flour and water until smooth. Gradually stir in broth. Bring to a boil; cook and stir 2 minutes or until thickened. Reduce heat; add soup, cheese and seasonings. Cook and stir 5 minutes or until cheese is melted.

3. Drain pasta; place in a bowl. Stir in soup mixture and chicken. Transfer to a greased 1½ qt. baking dish. Toss bread crumbs and butter; sprinkle over top. Bake, uncovered, 30 minutes or until golden brown.

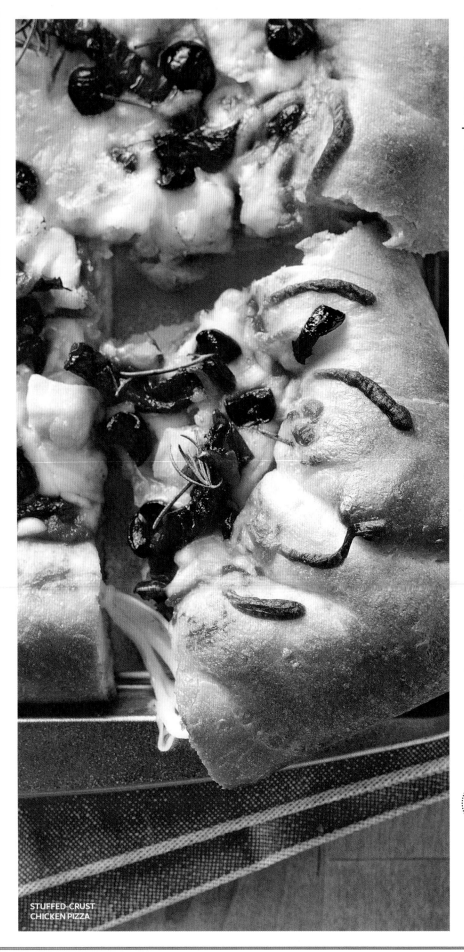

STUFFED-CRUST
CHICKEN PIZZA

Stuffed-Crust Chicken Pizza

Talk about a clever idea that just couldn't be quicker or easier! Convenient string cheese is the secret behind my yummy stuffed-crust chicken pizza.

—**PAM BROOKS** SOUTH BERWICK, ME

PREP: 35 MIN. • **BAKE:** 10 MIN.
MAKES: 12 PIECES

- 2 tubes (13.8 ounces each) refrigerated pizza crust
- 10 pieces string cheese
- ½ pound boneless skinless chicken breasts, cut into ½-inch cubes
- 1 small onion, chopped
- 2 tablespoons olive oil
- 3 garlic cloves, minced
- ½ cup oil-packed sun-dried tomatoes, julienned
- 1 teaspoon dried rosemary, crushed
- ½ teaspoon salt
- ½ teaspoon pepper
- ¾ cup pizza sauce
- 2 cups (8 ounces) shredded part-skim mozzarella cheese
- ½ cup pitted ripe olives, chopped

1. Unroll both pizza crusts and place in a greased 15-in. x 10-in. x 1-in. pan, letting dough drape 1 in. over the edges. Pinch center seam to seal.

2. Place string cheese around edges of pan. Fold dough over cheese; pinch to seal. Bake at 425° for 5 minutes.

3. Meanwhile, in a large skillet, saute chicken and onion in oil until chicken is no longer pink. Add garlic; cook 1 minute longer. Stir in the tomatoes, rosemary, salt and pepper.

4. Spread sauce over crust. Top with chicken mixture. Sprinkle with mozzarella and olives.

5. Bake for 10-15 minutes or until cheese is melted and crust is golden brown.

 **Did you know?**
Even though duck and geese breasts are darker than chicken and turkey breasts, they are still considered white meat. Duck and geese breasts are darker because these birds fly and use their breast muscles more than chickens.

FAVORITE CREAMY
CHICKEN CASSEROLE

Favorite Creamy Chicken Casserole

I created this when my husband was craving a dish his aunt used to make. It tastes and smells great and is now a staple in our house.

—MARI WARNKE FREMONT, WI

PREP: 20 MIN. • **BAKE:** 40 MIN.
MAKES: 2 CASSEROLES (5 SERVINGS EACH)

- 4 **cups uncooked egg noodles**
- 4 **cups cubed cooked chicken**
- 1 **package (16 ounces) frozen peas and carrots**
- 2 **cups milk**
- 2 **cans (10¾ ounces each) condensed cream of celery soup, undiluted**
- 2 **cans (10¾ ounces each) condensed cream of chicken soup, undiluted**
- 1 **cup chopped onion**
- 2 **tablespoons butter, melted**
- ½ **teaspoon salt**
- ½ **teaspoon pepper**

1. Preheat oven to 350°. Cook noodles according to package directions. Meanwhile, in a large bowl, combine the remaining ingredients. Drain noodles; add to chicken mixture.
2. Transfer to two greased 8-in. square baking dishes. Cover and bake 30 minutes. Uncover and bake 10-15 minutes longer or until heated through.

Pecan Oven-Fried Chicken

Pecans and a buttermilk baking mix give my Southern-style chicken a crispy coating that mimics the fried version.

—MILDRED TROUPE WARTRACE, TN

PREP: 10 MIN. • **BAKE:** 1 HOUR
MAKES: 4 SERVINGS

- 1½ **cups buttermilk baking mix**
- ¾ **cup finely chopped pecans**
- 1 **tablespoon paprika**
- 1½ **teaspoons salt**
- ¾ **teaspoon pepper**
- ¾ **teaspoon poultry seasoning**
- 1 **broiler/fryer chicken (3½ to 4 pounds), cut up**
- 1 **can (5 ounces) evaporated milk**
- ½ **cup butter, melted**

1. In a shallow bowl or large resealable plastic bag, combine baking mix, pecans, paprika, salt, pepper and poultry seasoning. Dip chicken pieces in milk, then coat generously with pecan mixture.
2. Place in a greased 13-in. x 9-in. baking dish. Drizzle with butter. Bake, uncovered, at 350° for 1 hour or until juices run clear.

Chicken Potpie

When you're craving comfort food, you can't go wrong with this choice. Bake one now and freeze the other for a time when a cozy meal is just what you're looking for.

—KAREN JOHNSON BAKERSFIELD, CA

PREP: 40 MIN. • **BAKE:** 35 MIN. + STANDING
MAKES: 2 POTPIES (8 SERVINGS EACH)

- 2 **cups diced peeled potatoes**
- 1¾ **cups sliced carrots**
- 1 **cup butter, cubed**
- ⅔ **cup chopped onion**
- 1 **cup all-purpose flour**
- 1¾ **teaspoons salt**
- 1 **teaspoon dried thyme**
- ¾ **teaspoon pepper**
- 3 **cups chicken broth**
- 1½ **cups milk**
- 4 **cups cubed cooked chicken**
- 1 **cup frozen peas**
- 1 **cup frozen corn**
- 2 **packages (14.1 ounces each) refrigerated pie pastry**

1. Preheat oven to 425°. Place potatoes and carrots in a large saucepan; add water to cover. Bring to a boil. Reduce heat; cook, covered, 8-10 minutes or until vegetables are crisp-tender; drain.
2. In a large skillet, heat butter over medium-high heat. Add onion; cook and stir until tender. Stir in flour and seasonings until blended. Gradually stir in broth and milk. Bring to a boil, stirring constantly; cook and stir 2 minutes or until thickened. Stir in chicken, peas, corn and potato mixture; remove from heat.
3. Unroll a pastry sheet into each of two 9-in. pie plates; trim even with rims. Add chicken mixture. Unroll remaining pastry; place over filling. Trim, seal and flute edges. Cut slits in tops.
4. Bake 35-40 minutes or until crust is lightly browned. Let stand 15 minutes before cutting.
Freeze option *Cover and freeze unbaked pies. To use, remove from freezer 30 minutes before baking (do not thaw). Preheat oven to 425°. Place pies on baking sheets; cover edges loosely with foil. Bake 30 minutes. Reduce oven setting to 350°; bake 70-80 minutes longer or until crust is golden brown and a thermometer inserted in center reads 165°.*

CHICKEN POTPIE

Texan Ranch Chicken Casserole

I'm happy this Texan Ranch Chicken Casserole was passed down to me because every time I make it, people rave about it. It's not too hot, so spice lovers can add jalapenos for more heat. I should note that it freezes well, too.

—**KENDRA DOSS** COLORADO SPRINGS, CO

PREP: 25 MIN. • **BAKE:** 30 MIN.
MAKES: 8 SERVINGS

- 1 **large onion, finely chopped**
- 2 **celery ribs, finely chopped**
- 1 **medium green pepper, finely chopped**
- 1 **medium sweet red pepper, finely chopped**
- 1 **tablespoon canola oil**
- 1 **garlic clove, minced**
- 3 **cups cubed cooked chicken breast**
- 1 **can (10¾ ounces) reduced-fat reduced-sodium condensed cream of celery soup, undiluted**
- 1 **can (10¾ ounces) reduced-fat reduced-sodium condensed cream of chicken soup, undiluted**
- 1 **can (10 ounces) diced tomatoes and green chilies, undrained**
- 1 **tablespoon chili powder**
- 12 **corn tortillas (6 inches), cut into 1-inch strips**
- 2 **cups (8 ounces) shredded reduced-fat cheddar cheese, divided**

1. In a large nonstick skillet coated with cooking spray, saute the onion, celery and peppers in oil until crisp-tender. Add garlic; cook 1 minute longer. Stir in the chicken, soups, tomatoes and chili powder.

2. Line the bottom of a 3-qt. baking dish with half of the tortilla strips; top with half of the chicken mixture and 1 cup cheese. Repeat layers. Bake, uncovered, at 350° for 30-35 minutes or until bubbly.

CURRIED COCONUT CHICKEN

TEXAN RANCH CHICKEN CASSEROLE

SERVES ②

Curried Coconut Chicken

Here's a five-ingredient recipe that's a nice change of pace. It's sweet, savory and a little exotic. Serve it over rice or couscous.

—**BECKY WALCH** MANTECA, CA

PREP: 10 MIN. • **BAKE:** 30 MIN.
MAKES: 2 SERVINGS

- 4 **teaspoons butter, melted**
- ½ **cup flaked coconut**
- 1 **teaspoon curry powder**
- 2 **boneless skinless chicken breast halves (6 ounces each)**
- ⅛ **teaspoon salt**
- ½ **cup apricot preserves, warmed**

1. Place butter in a shallow bowl. In another shallow bowl, combine the coconut and curry powder. Dip chicken in butter, then coat with coconut mixture.

2. Place in a greased 11-in. x 7-in. baking dish; sprinkle with salt. Bake, uncovered, at 350° for 30-35 minutes or until a meat thermometer reads 170°. Serve with preserves.

Southwestern Chicken Packets

Black beans, corn, salsa and a sprinkling of Mexican cheese add savory flavor to the juicy chicken in these oven-baked foil packets. But the best part is the easy clean-up.

—**TONYA VOWELS** VINE GROVE, KY

PREP: 10 MIN. • **BAKE:** 25 MIN.
MAKES: 4 SERVINGS

- 4 **boneless skinless chicken breast halves (4 ounces each)**
- ½ **teaspoon salt**
- ¼ **teaspoon pepper**
- ¾ **cup salsa**
- 2 **cups fresh or frozen corn, thawed**
- 1 **can (15 ounces) black beans, rinsed and drained**
- ¾ **cup shredded Mexican cheese blend**
- ¼ **cup sour cream**

1. Place each chicken breast half on a greased double thickness of heavy-duty foil (about 18 in. square). Sprinkle with salt and pepper. Top with salsa, corn, beans and cheese. Fold foil around mixture and seal tightly.
2. Place on a baking sheet. Bake at 425° for 25-30 minutes or until chicken juices run clear. Open foil carefully to allow steam to escape. Serve with sour cream.

Chicken with Corn Bread Stuffing

This is a simple and convenient dish that I can easily bake in our motor home's toaster oven. Even though it's quick, it tastes like a Thanksgiving dinner. We like it with sweet potatoes.

—**JOYCE MARTIN** CAMARILLO, CA

PREP: 20 MIN. • **BAKE:** 20 MIN.
MAKES: 2 SERVINGS

- 2 **boneless skinless chicken breast halves (5 ounces each)**
- 1½ **cups crushed corn bread stuffing, divided**
- 1 **medium tart apple, chopped**
- 4 **green onions, chopped**
- 2 **teaspoons canola oil**
- ¼ **teaspoon celery seed**

1. Flatten chicken to ½-in. thickness. Finely crush ¼ cup corn bread stuffing; place in a shallow bowl. Coat chicken with crumbs; set aside.
2. In a small skillet, saute apple and onions in oil until tender. Stir in celery seed and remaining corn bread stuffing. In a greased 11-in. x 7-in. baking dish, shape stuffing mixture into two oval mounds. Top each with a chicken breast.
3. Bake, uncovered, at 350° for 20-25 minutes or until a meat thermometer reads 170°.

Apple-Brined Chicken Thighs

I love the flavor of chicken baked with apples, and when I had a bumper crop of green beans, I wanted to include them, too. This recipe is the tasty result.

—**KATHY RAIRIGH** MILFORD, IN

PREP: 30 MIN. + CHILLING • **BAKE:** 55 MIN.
MAKES: 5 SERVINGS

- 3 **cups apple cider or juice**
- 1 **medium onion, sliced**
- 1 **medium lemon, sliced**
- 4 **fresh rosemary sprigs**
- ⅓ **cup kosher salt**
- ½ **cup packed brown sugar, divided**
- 4 **garlic cloves, minced**
- 1 **bay leaf**
- 1 **teaspoon whole peppercorns**
- 2 **cups cold water**

APPLE-BRINED
CHICKEN THIGHS

- 10 **bone-in chicken thighs (about 3¾ pounds)**
  One 2-gallon resealable plastic bag
- 1 **pound fresh green beans, trimmed**
- 3 **medium tart apples, cut into wedges**
- 1 **tablespoon minced fresh rosemary or 1 teaspoon dried rosemary, crushed**
- 1 **tablespoon olive oil**
- ¼ **teaspoon pepper**

1. In a Dutch oven, combine the cider, onion, lemon, rosemary sprigs, salt, ¼ cup brown sugar, garlic, bay leaf and peppercorns. Bring to a boil. Cook and stir until salt and brown sugar are dissolved. Remove from the heat; stir in water. Cool brine to room temperature.
2. Place chicken in the 2-gallon resealable plastic bag. Carefully pour cooled brine into bag. Squeeze out as much air as possible; seal bag and turn to coat. Place in a roasting pan. Refrigerate for 2 hours, turning occasionally.
3. Place beans and apples in a greased roasting pan. Drain chicken; place in prepared pan. Bake, uncovered, at 400° for 40 minutes.
4. Combine the minced rosemary, oil, pepper and remaining brown sugar; sprinkle over chicken. Bake 15-25 minutes longer or until a thermometer reads 180° and beans are tender.

CHICKEN AND
SAUSAGE MANICOTTI

Chicken & Sausage Manicotti

This recipe makes two tasty, cheesy casseroles. You can serve one tonight and freeze the second one for later.

—FRAN SCOTT BIRMINGHAM, MI

PREP: 30 MIN. • **BAKE:** 55 MIN. + STANDING
MAKES: 2 CASSEROLES (7 SERVINGS EACH)

- 1 **pound sliced fresh mushrooms**
- 2 **medium green peppers, chopped**
- 2 **medium onions, chopped**
- 1 **tablespoon olive oil**
- 4 **garlic cloves, minced**
- 3 **jars (26 ounces each) spaghetti sauce**
- 1¼ **cups water**
- 1½ **pounds chicken tenderloins, halved lengthwise**
- 4 **teaspoons dried basil**
- 2 **teaspoons chicken seasoning**
- 2 **packages (8 ounces each) uncooked manicotti shells**
- 1 **pound fully cooked andouille or Italian sausage links, halved lengthwise and sliced**
- 2 **cups (8 ounces) shredded part-skim mozzarella cheese**
- 2 **cups (8 ounces) shredded cheddar cheese**

1. In a Dutch oven, saute mushrooms, peppers and onions in oil until tender. Add garlic; cook 1 minute longer. Stir in spaghetti sauce and water.
2. Sprinkle chicken with basil and chicken seasoning. Stuff chicken into uncooked manicotti shells. Spread 1 cup sauce mixture in each of two greased 13-in. x 9-in. baking dishes.

For Two

If a recipe calls for a 13- x 9-inch baking dish, I reduce the ingredients by half and divide the mixture into two 1-quart dishes. The shallower fill makes it the perfect size meal for my husband and me. I bake one casserole for dinner and keep the other in the freezer for another meal.

—LAURA KITTLESON SANDY, UT

Arrange manicotti over sauce; sprinkle with sausage. Pour remaining sauce over top; sprinkle with cheeses.
3. Cover and freeze one casserole for up to 3 months. Cover and bake the remaining casserole at 375° for 55-65 minutes or until bubbly and pasta is tender. Let stand for 10 minutes before serving.
To use frozen manicotti *Thaw in the refrigerator overnight. Remove from the refrigerator 30 minutes before baking. Cover and bake at 375° for 55-65 minutes or until chicken and pasta are tender. Let stand for 10 minutes before serving.*

Summer Squash Chicken Casserole

In summer, we love to try new recipes that feature pattypan squash. This protein-packed dish turned out rich and saucy, and each serving is less than 300 calories.

—TASTE OF HOME TEST KITCHEN

PREP: 20 MIN. • **BAKE:** 30 MIN.
MAKES: 6 SERVINGS

- ½ **cup uncooked instant rice**
- 1 **can (10¾ ounces) condensed cream of chicken soup, undiluted**
- ⅓ **cup reduced-fat mayonnaise**
- ⅓ **cup fat-free milk**
- 4 **cups cubed cooked chicken breast**
- 2 **cups pattypan squash, halved**
- 1 **small onion, finely chopped**
- 1 **jar (2 ounces) diced pimientos, drained**
- 1 **teaspoon dried thyme**
- ¼ **teaspoon garlic powder**
- ¼ **teaspoon pepper**
- ⅓ **cup shredded Parmesan cheese**

1. Cook rice according to package directions. In a large bowl, combine the soup, mayonnaise and milk. Stir in the chicken, squash, onion, pimientos, thyme, garlic powder, pepper and cooked rice.
2. Spoon into a 2-qt. baking dish coated with cooking spray. Sprinkle with cheese. Bake, uncovered, at 350° for 30-40 minutes or until edges are bubbly and center is set.

Chicken Dinner Packets

The chicken stays nice and juicy in this meal-in-one packet. I especially like this entree because it saves so much time, and the dishes are done in a flash!

—JEANNE BARNEY SARATOGA SPRINGS, NY

PREP: 15 MIN. • **BAKE:** 25 MIN.
MAKES: 2 SERVINGS

- ½ **pound boneless skinless chicken breasts, cut into strips**
- 2 **small red potatoes, thinly sliced**
- ¾ **cup shredded cheddar cheese**
- ½ **small sweet red pepper, julienned**
- ½ **small green pepper, julienned**
- 2 **tablespoons barbecue sauce**
- 1 **green onion, chopped**
- ¼ **teaspoon salt**
- ⅛ **teaspoon pepper**

1. Divide chicken strips between two pieces of heavy-duty foil (about 12 in. square). In a small bowl, combine the remaining ingredients; spoon over chicken. Fold foil around mixture and seal tightly.
2. Place packets on a baking sheet. Bake at 375° for 25-30 minutes or until chicken is no longer pink and potatoes are tender. Open foil carefully to allow steam to escape.

CHICKEN DINNER PACKETS

Thai Chicken Pizza

START TO FINISH: 25 MIN. • **MAKES:** 6 SERVINGS

- 1 prebaked 12-inch pizza crust
- ⅔ cup Thai peanut sauce
- 2 tablespoons reduced-sodium soy sauce
- 2 tablespoons creamy peanut butter
- 1 cup shredded cooked chicken breast
- 1 cup (4 ounces) shredded part-skim mozzarella cheese
- 3 green onions, chopped
- ½ cup bean sprouts
- ½ cup shredded carrot

1. Place crust on an ungreased 12-in. pizza pan or baking sheet. In a small bowl, combine the peanut sauce, soy sauce and peanut butter. Add chicken; toss to coat. Spread over crust; sprinkle with cheese and onions.
2. Bake at 400° for 10-12 minutes or until cheese is melted. Top with bean sprouts and carrot.

This is a recipe I made for my friends on a girl's night filled with fun and laughter. It is simple to make but full of flavor.

—**KIMBERLY KNUPPENBURG** MENOMONEE FALLS, WI

THAI CHICKEN PIZZA

BALSAMIC ROAST CHICKEN

Balsamic Roast Chicken

Balsamic, wine and rosemary are classic flavors that work well together. This recipe has the makings for a special Sunday dinner with friends and family.

—**TRACY TYLKOWSKI** OMAHA, NE

PREP: 20 MIN. • **BAKE:** 2¼ HOURS + STANDING
MAKES: 12 SERVINGS (1½ CUPS ONION SAUCE)

- 1 roasting chicken (6 to 7 pounds)
- 2 tablespoons minced fresh rosemary or 2 teaspoons dried rosemary, crushed
- 3 garlic cloves, minced
- 1 teaspoon salt
- 1 teaspoon pepper
- 2 medium red onions, chopped
- ½ cup dry red wine or reduced-sodium chicken broth
- ½ cup balsamic vinegar

1. Pat chicken dry. In a small bowl, combine the rosemary, garlic, salt and pepper; rub under skin of chicken. Place onions in a shallow roasting pan; top with chicken. Combine wine and balsamic vinegar; pour over chicken.
2. Bake, uncovered, at 350° for 2¼ to 2¾ hours or until a meat thermometer reads 180°, basting occasionally with pan juices. (Cover loosely with foil if chicken browns too quickly.)
3. Let stand for 15 minutes before carving. Remove and discard skin before serving. Pour onion sauce into a small bowl; skim fat. Serve with chicken.

Chicken & Pear Bundles

Filled with smoked mozzarella and sweet pears, these creative bundles are elegance at its easiest. A simple raspberry sauce finishes the dish nicely.
—**TASTE OF HOME TEST KITCHEN**

PREP: 20 MIN. • **BAKE:** 20 MIN. • **MAKES:** 4 SERVINGS

- 4 **boneless skinless chicken breast halves (5 ounces each)**
- ¼ **teaspoon salt**
- ¼ **teaspoon pepper**
- 1 **sheet frozen puff pastry, thawed**
- 4 **slices smoked mozzarella cheese**
- 2 **medium ripe pears, thinly sliced**
- 1 **egg, beaten**
- ½ **cup seedless raspberry preserves**
- 1 **teaspoon cider vinegar**

1. Flatten chicken breasts evenly; sprinkle with salt and pepper. On a lightly floured surface, roll pastry sheet into a 14-in. square. Cut into four squares. Place a chicken breast in the center of each square; top each with cheese and pear slices.

2. Lightly brush pastry edges with egg. Bring opposite corners of pastry over each bundle; pinch seams to seal. Place seam side down on a greased baking sheet; brush with remaining egg.

3. Bake at 400° for 20-25 minutes or until golden brown and a meat thermometer reads 170°.

4. In a small microwave-safe bowl, combine preserves and vinegar. Microwave, uncovered, on high for 20-25 seconds or until melted. Serve with bundles.

CHICKEN & PEAR BUNDLES

ROSEMARY LEMON CHICKEN

Rosemary Lemon Chicken

I'm a busy mom of four and a nursing student, so weeknight dinners are often rushed. Sunday dinners are very important to our family and everyone loves when I make this old-fashioned chicken recipe.
—**AMY JENKINS** MESA, AZ

PREP: 40 MIN. • **BAKE:** 2¼ HOURS + STANDING
MAKES: 6 SERVINGS

- 2 **to 3 medium lemons**
- 2 **fresh rosemary sprigs**
- 1 **roasting chicken (6 to 7 pounds)**
- 1 **tablespoon olive oil**
- 2 **tablespoons minced fresh rosemary**
- 1 **tablespoon coarsely ground pepper**
- 1½ **teaspoons salt**

1. Finely grate the peel from the lemons to measure 2 tablespoons; set aside. Coarsely chop 2 lemons; place chopped lemons and rosemary sprigs in the chicken cavity. Save remaining lemon for another use.

2. Place chicken on a rack in a shallow roasting pan; brush with oil. Combine the minced rosemary, pepper, salt and lemon peel; rub over chicken.

3. Bake, uncovered, at 350° for 2¼ to 2¾ hours or until a thermometer reads 180°, basting occasionally with drippings. (Cover loosely with foil if chicken browns too quickly.)

4. Let stand for 15 minutes before carving. Discard lemons and rosemary sprigs.

Chicken & Spaghetti Squash

While dreaming up a healthier pasta dish, I decided to experiment with spaghetti squash. After a few tries, I settled on this entree that's bursting with flavor, without a lot of fat.

—CHRISTINA MORRIS CALABASAS, CA

PREP: 45 MIN. • **BAKE:** 20 MIN.
MAKES: 5 SERVINGS

- 1 medium spaghetti squash (4 pounds)
- 1 can (14½ ounces) diced tomatoes, undrained
- 2 tablespoons prepared pesto
- ½ teaspoon garlic powder
- ½ teaspoon Italian seasoning
- ¼ cup dry bread crumbs
- ¼ cup shredded Parmesan cheese
- 1 pound boneless skinless chicken breasts, cut into ½-inch cubes
- 1 tablespoon plus 1 teaspoon olive oil, divided
- ½ pound sliced fresh mushrooms
- 1 medium onion, chopped
- 1 garlic clove, minced
- ½ cup chicken broth
- ⅓ cup shredded cheddar cheese

1. Cut squash in half lengthwise; discard seeds. Place squash cut side down on a microwave-safe plate. Microwave, uncovered, on high for 14-16 minutes or until tender.
2. Meanwhile, in a blender, combine the tomatoes, pesto, garlic powder and Italian seasoning. Cover and process until blended; set aside. In a small bowl, combine bread crumbs and Parmesan cheese; set aside.
3. In a large skillet, cook chicken in 1 tablespoon oil until no longer pink; remove and keep warm. In the same skillet, saute mushrooms and onion in remaining oil until tender. Add garlic; cook 1 minute longer. Stir in the broth, chicken and reserved tomato mixture. Bring to a boil. Reduce heat; simmer, uncovered, for 5 minutes.
4. When the squash is cool enough to handle, use a fork to separate strands. In a large ovenproof skillet, layer half of the squash, chicken mixture and reserved crumb mixture. Repeat layers.
5. Bake, uncovered, at 350° for 15 minutes or until heated through. Sprinkle with cheddar cheese. Broil 3-4 in. from the heat for 5-6 minutes or until cheese is melted and golden brown.
NOTE *This recipe was tested in a 1,100-watt microwave.*

SERVES ②

Simple Southwest Chicken

One evening I decided to spice up our chicken while baking plain chicken for the kids. My husband liked it so much that it's become a regular dinner in our home.

JAN COOPER TROY, AL

PREP: 10 MIN. • **BAKE:** 25 MIN.
MAKES: 2 SERVINGS

- 2 boneless skinless chicken breast halves (5 ounces each)
- ⅛ teaspoon salt
- ⅓ cup salsa
- 2 tablespoons taco sauce
- ⅓ cup shredded reduced-fat Mexican cheese blend

1. Place chicken in a shallow 2-qt. baking dish coated with cooking spray. Sprinkle with salt. Combine salsa and taco sauce; drizzle over chicken. Sprinkle with cheese.
2. Cover and bake at 350° for 25-30 minutes or until the chicken juices run clear.

CREAMY OLIVE-STUFFED CHICKEN

Creamy Olive-Stuffed Chicken

Guess what? This 6-ingredient stuffed chicken entree is not only a cinch to prepare, it's good for you, too. In less than an hour, you can have dinner on the table and feel good knowing that each serving has less than 300 calories.

—TASTE OF HOME TEST KITCHEN

PREP: 20 MIN. • **BAKE:** 20 MIN.
MAKES: 4 SERVINGS

- 4 boneless skinless chicken breast halves (6 ounces each)
- 4 ounces fat-free cream cheese
- 1 can (2¼ ounces) sliced ripe olives, drained
- ⅛ teaspoon dried oregano
- ⅛ teaspoon pepper
- ½ cup seasoned bread crumbs
- 1 tablespoon olive oil

1. Preheat oven to 350°. Flatten chicken to ¼-in. thickness. In a small bowl, combine cream cheese, olives, oregano and pepper. Spoon 2 tablespoons down center of each chicken breast. Fold chicken over filling; secure with toothpicks, then roll in bread crumbs.
2. In a large oven-proof skillet, brown chicken in oil. Bake 20-25 minutes or until juices run clear. Discard toothpicks.

CHICKEN AND SPAGHETTI SQUASH

Lemon & Sage Roasted Chicken

Aromatic scents of lemon and garlic will draw the whole family to the table, and it's worth every minute of the wait.

—**JAN VALDEZ** CHICAGO, IL

PREP: 20 MIN. + MARINATING
BAKE: 2¼ HOURS + STANDING
MAKES: 6 SERVINGS

- ¼ cup lemon juice
- ¼ cup plus 3 tablespoons olive oil, divided
- 5 garlic cloves, minced
- 2 tablespoons minced fresh sage
- 1 roasting chicken (6 to 7 pounds)
- 2 tablespoons butter, softened
- 1 medium lemon, cut into wedges
- 8 medium potatoes, quartered
- 2 medium onions, quartered
- ½ teaspoon salt
- ¼ teaspoon pepper

1. In a 2-gallon resealable plastic bag, combine the lemon juice, ¼ cup oil, garlic and sage. Add the chicken; seal bag and turn to coat. Refrigerate for at least 4 hours. Drain and discard marinade.

2. With fingers, carefully loosen skin from the chicken; rub butter under the skin. Fill cavity with lemon wedges. Place chicken breast side up on a rack in a roasting pan.

3. In a large bowl, combine the potatoes, onions, salt, pepper and remaining oil. Arrange around chicken. Bake, uncovered, at 350° for 2¼ to 2¾ hours or until a thermometer reads 180°. Cover loosely with foil if chicken browns too quickly. Let stand for 15 minutes before carving.

LEMON AND SAGE ROASTED CHICKEN

SALSA VERDE CHICKEN CASSEROLE

Salsa Verde Chicken Casserole

Here's a rich and tasty rendition of all my favorite Tex-Mex dishes rolled into one beautiful casserole. Best of all, it's ready in no time!

—**JANET MCCORMICK** PROCTORVILLE, OH

START TO FINISH: 30 MIN.
MAKES: 6 SERVINGS

- 2 cups shredded rotisserie chicken
- 1 cup (8 ounces) sour cream
- 1½ cups salsa verde, divided
- 8 corn tortillas (6 inches)
- 2 cups chopped tomatoes
- ¼ cup minced fresh cilantro
- 2 cups (8 ounces) shredded Monterey Jack cheese
  Optional toppings: avocado slices, thinly sliced green onions or fresh cilantro leaves

1. Combine the chicken, sour cream and ¾ cup salsa in a small bowl. Spread ¼ cup salsa on the bottom of a greased 8-in. square baking dish.

2. Layer half of the tortillas and chicken mixture; sprinkle with the tomatoes, minced cilantro and half of the cheese. Repeat layers with remaining tortillas, chicken mixture and cheese.

3. Bake, uncovered, at 400° for 20-25 minutes or until bubbly. Serve with remaining salsa and, if desired, optional toppings.

Alfredo Chicken Lasagna

I came up with this recipe after trying something similar in a restaurant. This version serves 2 or 3.

—BRIDGETTE MONAGHAN MASONVILLE, IA

PREP: 25 MIN. • **BAKE:** 40 MIN. + STANDING
MAKES: 3 SERVINGS

- 6 ounces boneless skinless chicken breast, cut into bite-size pieces
- 1 cup sliced fresh mushrooms
- 2 tablespoons chopped onion
- 1 tablespoon olive oil
- 1 garlic clove, minced
- 1 tablespoon all-purpose flour
- 1 cup Alfredo sauce
- ¾ cup 2% cottage cheese
- ¼ cup plus 2 tablespoons shredded Parmesan cheese, divided
- 1 egg, lightly beaten
- ½ teaspoon Italian seasoning
- ½ teaspoon dried parsley flakes
- 4 lasagna noodles, cooked and drained
- 1½ cups (6 ounces) shredded part-skim mozzarella cheese

1. In a large skillet, saute the chicken, mushrooms and onion in oil until chicken is no longer pink. Add garlic; cook 1 minute longer. Stir in flour until blended; gradually stir in Alfredo sauce. Bring to a boil. Reduce heat; simmer, uncovered, for 3-5 minutes or until thickened.

2. In a small bowl, combine the cottage cheese, ¼ cup Parmesan cheese, egg, Italian seasoning and parsley.

3. Spread ½ cup Alfredo mixture in an 8-in. x 4-in. loaf pan coated with cooking spray. Layer with two noodles (trimmed to fit pan), half of the cottage cheese mixture, half of the remaining Alfredo mixture and ¾ cup mozzarella cheese. Sprinkle with remaining Parmesan cheese. Repeat layers.

4. Cover and bake at 350° for 30 minutes. Uncover; bake 10 minutes longer or until bubbly. Let stand for 10 minutes before cutting.

ALFREDO CHICKEN LASAGNA

Chicken Biscuit Bake

This recipe looks fussy but doesn't take long to assemble. Plus, it gives me time to put my feet up and read the paper while it bakes. I like to keep things simple by serving it with salad and some fruit.

—GAIL CORY-BETZ NEWPORT, WA

PREP: 20 MIN. • **BAKE:** 30 MIN.
MAKES: 2 SERVINGS

- ½ cup plus 1 tablespoon all-purpose flour
- ½ teaspoon baking powder
  Dash salt
- 3 tablespoons cold butter
- 2 tablespoons beaten egg
- ¼ cup buttermilk

FILLING

- 2 tablespoons butter
- 2 tablespoons all-purpose flour
- 1 cup 2% milk
- 1 tablespoon chicken bouillon granules
  Dash poultry seasoning
  Dash onion powder
- ½ cup cubed cooked chicken
- ½ cup frozen mixed vegetables
- ½ cup 4% cottage cheese

1. In a small bowl, combine the flour, baking powder and salt; cut in butter until mixture resembles coarse crumbs. Set aside 1 teaspoon beaten egg; stir remaining egg into buttermilk. Add to crumb mixture; stir until dough forms a ball.

2. Turn onto a floured surface; knead 10 times or until smooth. Divide the dough in half. On a lightly floured surface, roll out one portion to fit the bottom of a greased 1-qt. baking dish. Place in dish.

3. In a small saucepan, melt butter over medium heat. Stir in flour until smooth. Gradually add the milk, bouillon, poultry seasoning and onion powder. Bring to a boil; cook and stir for 1-2 minutes or until thickened. Remove from the heat. Stir in the chicken, vegetables and cottage cheese. Pour into baking dish.

4. Roll out remaining dough to fit top of dish; place over filling. Brush with reserved egg. Bake at 350° for 30-35 minutes or until golden brown.

ROAST CHICKEN BREASTS
WITH PEPPERS

Chicken Provolone

Chicken Provolone, though one of my simplest dishes, is also one of my husband's favorites. It's easy to prepare and looks fancy served with a garnish of fresh parsley or thinly sliced basil.

—**DAWN E. BRYANT** THEDFORD, NE

START TO FINISH: 25 MIN.
MAKES: 4 SERVINGS

- 4 **boneless skinless chicken breast halves (4 ounces each)**
- ¼ **teaspoon pepper**
  Butter-flavored cooking spray
- 8 **fresh basil leaves**
- 4 **thin slices prosciutto or deli ham**
- 4 **slices provolone cheese**

1. Sprinkle chicken with pepper. In a large nonstick skillet coated with butter-flavored cooking spray, cook chicken over medium heat for 4-5 minutes on each side or until a thermometer reads 170°.
2. Transfer to an ungreased baking sheet; top with the basil, prosciutto and cheese. Broil 6-8 in. from the heat for 1-2 minutes or until cheese is melted.

Roast Chicken Breasts with Peppers

I'm in love with this dish because it goes from start to finish in nearly no time.

—**MELISSA GALINAT** LAKELAND, FL

START TO FINISH: 30 MIN.
MAKES: 4 SERVINGS

- ¾ **teaspoon fennel seed, crushed**
- ¾ **teaspoon salt, divided**
- ½ **teaspoon pepper, divided**
- ¼ **teaspoon garlic powder**
- ¼ **teaspoon dried oregano**
- 4 **boneless skinless chicken breast halves (5 ounces each)**
- 2 **teaspoons plus 1 tablespoon olive oil, divided**
- 1 **large sweet red pepper, thinly sliced**
- 1 **medium sweet yellow pepper, thinly sliced**
- 4 **shallots, thinly sliced**
- 1 **cup chicken broth**
- 1½ **teaspoons minced fresh rosemary**
- 1 **tablespoon balsamic vinegar**

1. In a large dry skillet, toast the fennel, ½ teaspoon salt, ¼ teaspoon pepper, garlic powder and oregano over medium heat for 1-2 minutes or until aromatic, stirring frequently. Cool slightly. Sprinkle over chicken.
2. In the same skillet, heat 2 teaspoons oil over medium-high heat. Brown chicken, about 2 minutes on each side. Transfer to an ungreased 15-in. x 10-in. x 1-in. baking pan. Bake at 450° for 10-15 minutes or until a thermometer reads 170°.
3. Meanwhile, heat remaining oil in the same skillet. Add peppers and shallots; cook and stir over medium heat until crisp-tender.
4. Add broth and rosemary, stirring to loosen browned bits from pan. Bring to a boil; cook for 4-6 minutes or until broth is almost evaporated. Stir in vinegar and remaining salt and pepper. Serve with chicken.

CHICKEN PROVOLONE

WEST COAST CHICKEN

Creamy Chicken Enchiladas

My daughter brought 10 pans of these yummy enchiladas to my wedding reception, and it was the biggest hit of all the food. Because so many people wanted the recipe, we sent it out with our Christmas cards.

—**PAT COFFEE** KINGSTON, WA

PREP: 30 MIN. • **BAKE:** 35 MIN. • **MAKES:** 10 SERVINGS

- 1 package (8 ounces) cream cheese, softened
- 2 tablespoons water
- 2 teaspoons onion powder
- 2 teaspoons ground cumin
- ½ teaspoon salt
- ¼ teaspoon pepper
- 5 cups diced cooked chicken
- 20 flour tortillas (6 inches), room temperature
- 2 cans (10¾ ounces each) condensed cream of chicken soup, undiluted
- 2 cups (16 ounces) sour cream
- 1 cup 2% milk
- 2 cans (4 ounces each) chopped green chilies
- 2 cups (8 ounces) shredded cheddar cheese

1. In a large bowl, beat the cream cheese, water, onion powder, cumin, salt and pepper until smooth. Stir in the chicken.
2. Place ¼ cup chicken mixture down the center of each tortilla. Roll up and place seam side down in two greased 13-in. x 9-in. baking dishes. In a large bowl, combine the soup, sour cream, milk and chilies; pour over enchiladas.
3. Bake, uncovered, at 350° for 30-40 minutes or until heated through. Sprinkle with cheese; bake 5 minutes longer or until cheese is melted.

West Coast Chicken

We're far from the West Coast, but the orange and ginger in the sauce for this chicken give us a taste of that part of the country. And it's one we enjoy frequently...my family wouldn't mind if I served this dish a couple of times every week.

—**DENISE HOPPER** LOGAN, OH

PREP: 15 MIN. + MARINATING • **BAKE:** 1 HOUR
MAKES: 8 SERVINGS

- 1 cup thawed orange juice concentrate
- ⅓ cup butter, melted
- 4 teaspoons soy sauce
- 2 teaspoons salt
- 2 teaspoons ground ginger
- ¼ teaspoon pepper
- 5 pounds bone-in chicken thighs, skin removed

1. In a small bowl, combine the first six ingredients. Place chicken in a single layer in two greased 11-in. x 7-in. baking dishes; spoon sauce over the top. Cover and refrigerate overnight.
2. Remove from the refrigerator 30 minutes before baking. Bake, uncovered, at 350° for 1 hour or until juices run clear, basting with sauce once with during cooking.

CREAMY CHICKEN ENCHILADAS

MALIBU CHICKEN BUNDLES

Malibu Chicken Bundles

This was an instant hit the first time I made it and we agreed I wouldn't change a thing about the recipe. Mustard may seem like an odd ingredient, but it adds a nice touch.
—**BEVERLY NORRIS** EVANSTON, WY

PREP: 25 MIN. • **BAKE:** 45 MIN. • **MAKES:** 4 SERVINGS

 4 boneless skinless chicken breast halves (4 ounces each)
 ½ cup honey Dijon mustard, divided
 4 thin slices deli ham
 4 slices reduced-fat Swiss cheese
 1 can (8 ounces) unsweetened crushed pineapple, well drained
 1½ cups panko (Japanese) bread crumbs
 ¼ teaspoon salt
 ¼ teaspoon pepper
SAUCE
 1 can (10¾ ounces) reduced-fat reduced-sodium condensed cream of chicken soup, undiluted
 ¼ cup reduced-fat sour cream
 ⅛ teaspoon dried tarragon

1. Flatten chicken breasts to ¼-in. thickness. Spread 1 tablespoon mustard over each; layer with ham, cheese and pineapple. Fold chicken over pineapple; secure with toothpicks. Brush bundles with remaining mustard.
2. In a shallow bowl, combine the bread crumbs, salt and pepper. Roll bundles in bread crumb mixture; place in an 11-in. x 7-in. baking dish coated with cooking spray. Bake, uncovered, at 350° for 45-50 minutes or until a meat thermometer reads 170°. Discard toothpicks.
3. Meanwhile, in a small saucepan, combine the sauce ingredients. Cook, stirring occasionally, until heated through. Serve with chicken.

Chicken Lasagna Roll-Ups

PREP: 35 MIN. • **BAKE:** 45 MIN. • **MAKES:** 10 SERVINGS

 10 lasagna noodles
 ¾ pound boneless skinless chicken breasts, cubed
 1½ teaspoons herbes de Provence
 ½ teaspoon salt, divided
 ½ teaspoon pepper, divided
 1 tablespoon olive oil
 2 cups ricotta cheese
 ½ cup grated Parmesan cheese, divided
 ¼ cup 2% milk
 2 tablespoons minced fresh parsley
 4 cups spaghetti sauce
 8 ounces fresh mozzarella cheese, thinly sliced

1. Cook lasagna noodles according to package directions.
2. Meanwhile, sprinkle chicken with herbs de Provence, ¼ teaspoon salt and ¼ teaspoon pepper. In a large skillet, cook chicken in oil over medium heat for 5-7 minutes or until no longer pink; set aside.
3. In a large bowl, combine the ricotta, ¼ cup Parmesan cheese, milk, parsley and remaining salt and pepper. Add the chicken.
4. Drain noodles. Spread 1 cup spaghetti sauce into a greased 13-in. x 9-in. baking dish. Spread ⅓ cup chicken mixture over each noodle; carefully roll up. Place seam side down over sauce. Top with remaining sauce and Parmesan cheese.
5. Cover and bake at 375° for 30 minutes. Uncover; top with mozzarella cheese. Bake 15-20 minutes longer or until bubbly and cheese is melted.
NOTE *Look for herbes de Provence in the spice aisle.*

 I love to experiment wth new pasta dishes. Ingredients I had on hand and frozen sauce led to these tasty lasagna-flavored roll-ups. —**CYNDY GERKEN** NAPLES, FL

Sweet Salsa Chicken

I love finding good, healthy recipes, so I thought I should share this low-fat dinner my family loves. It's one of our favorites!

—**JOANNE WATTERS** COBOURG, ON

PREP: 20 MIN. + MARINATING
BAKE: 20MIN. • **MAKES:** 6 SERVINGS

- 1½ cups salsa
- ⅔ cup honey
- ½ cup orange juice
- ½ cup reduced-sodium soy sauce
- ¼ cup Dijon mustard
- 4 teaspoons olive oil
- ½ teaspoon ground ginger
- 6 boneless skinless chicken breast halves (4 ounces each)
- 1½ teaspoons cornstarch
- 2 tablespoons cold water

1. In a small bowl, combine the first seven ingredients. Pour 1½ cups into a large resealable plastic bag; add the chicken. Seal bag and turn to coat; refrigerate for 2 hours. Cover and refrigerate remaining marinade.
2. Drain and discard marinade from chicken. Place the chicken in an 11-in. x 7-in. baking dish coated with cooking spray; top with reserved marinade.

SWEET SALSA CHICKEN

3. Bake, uncovered, at 375° for 20-25 minutes or until a meat thermometer reads 180° Remove the chicken and keep warm.
4. In a small saucepan, combine cornstarch and cold water until smooth; stir in pan juices. Bring to a boil; cook and stir for 2 minutes or until thickened. Serve with chicken.

Chicken 'n' Rice Hot Dish

This is one of those comforting, simple dishes that needs only a salad and some bread to make a complete meal. I love to serve this to guests.

—**FAYE LABATT** MINNEAPOLIS, MN

PREP: 15 MIN. • **BAKE:** 30 MIN.
MAKES: 4 SERVINGS

- ½ cup uncooked instant brown rice
- ¼ cup boiling water
- 1 package (10 ounces) frozen chopped spinach, thawed and squeezed dry
- 1 tablespoon butter
- 3 tablespoons all-purpose flour
- ½ teaspoon curry powder
- ¼ teaspoon salt
  Dash pepper
  Dash garlic powder
- ¾ cup reduced-sodium chicken broth
- ¾ cup fat-free milk
- ¼ cup reduced-fat mayonnaise
- 3 cups cubed cooked chicken breast
- ⅓ cup shredded Parmesan cheese

1. Combine rice and water; transfer to an 11-in. x 7-in. baking dish coated with cooking spray. Top with spinach.
2. In a nonstick saucepan coated with cooking spray, melt butter. Stir in the flour, curry, salt, pepper and garlic powder until blended. Gradually whisk in broth and milk until smooth. Bring to a boil; cook and stir for 2 minutes or until thickened.
3. Remove from the heat; whisk in mayonnaise until blended. Pour half of the sauce over spinach. Top with chicken and remaining sauce.
4. Cover and bake at 350° for 25 minutes. Uncover; sprinkle with Parmesan cheese. Bake 5-10 minutes longer or until heated through and rice is tender.

HONEY MUSTARD CHICKEN

Honey Mustard Chicken

You can't go wrong with a classic combination of honey and mustard, but if you want to spice things up a bit, try different styles of mustard, like Dijon or hot Chinese.

—**RICHARD GALLOP** PUEBLO, CO

PREP: 15 MIN. • **BAKE:** 45 MIN.
MAKES: 6 SERVINGS

- ½ cup honey
- ¼ cup prepared mustard
- 1 envelope ranch salad dressing mix
- 1 tablespoon dried parsley flakes
- 1½ teaspoons Italian seasoning
- ½ teaspoon dried basil
- ½ teaspoon chili powder
- ¼ teaspoon garlic powder
- ¼ teaspoon pepper
- 6 chicken drumsticks
- 6 bone-in chicken thighs

1. For sauce, in a small bowl, combine the first nine ingredients. Set aside ½ cup for serving. Place chicken in a greased 15-in. x 10-in. x 1-in. baking pan; drizzle with remaining sauce.
2. Bake, uncovered, at 350° for 45-50 minutes or until a meat thermometer reads 180°, basting occasionally with pan juices. Warm reserved sauce; serve with chicken.

Buying whole chickens and cutting them each into 8 parts is an affordable way to get dinner on the table. Here's how:

❶ Pull the leg and thigh away from the body. With a small sharp knife, cut through the skin to expose the joint.

❷ Cut through joint, then cut skin around thigh to free leg. Repeat with other leg.

❸ Separate drumstick from thigh by cutting skin at the joint. Bend drumstick to expose joint, cut through joint and skin.

❹ Pull wing away from the body. Cut through skin to expose joint. Cut through joint and skin to separate wing from body. Repeat.

❺ Cut through the ribs along each side of the backbone with kitchen or poultry shears; discard backbone.

❻ Hold chicken breast in both hands (skin side down) and bend it back to snap breastbone. Turn over. With a knife, cut in half along breastbone. Breastbone will remain attached to one of the halves.

Glazed Chicken with Lemon Relish

I love to cook with herbs and citrus fruits, and this zesty lemon relish is the ideal condiment for my glazed chicken.

—**DIANE HIXON** NICEVILLE, FL

PREP: 10 MIN. • **BROIL:** 25 MIN.
MAKES: 4-6 SERVINGS
(ABOUT ¾ CUP RELISH)

- ⅓ cup chicken broth
- ¼ cup butter
- ¼ cup chopped onion
- 1 tablespoon honey
- 1 teaspoon dried thyme
- ½ teaspoon salt
- ⅛ teaspoon pepper
- 1 broiler/fryer chicken (about 3 pounds), cut in pieces

LEMON RELISH
- 1 lemon
- ½ celery rib, cut up
- ¼ small sweet red pepper, cut up
- 2 green onion, cut up
- 1½ teaspoons sugar
- ½ teaspoon salt
- ¼ teaspoon hot pepper sauce

1. In a saucepan, combine the first seven ingredients; bring to a boil. Reduce heat and simmer, uncovered, for 5 minutes.

2. Remove from the heat. Dip chicken pieces in glaze; place on broiler rack. Broil, approximately 5 in. from the heat, for 12 minutes, basting several times with the glaze. turn chicken; broil 10-12 minutes more or until done.

3. Meanwhile, trim outer portion of peel from lemon; set aside. Cut off and discard white membrane. Quarter lemon; discard seeds. Place lemon and peel in a food processor or blender; process until peel is finely chopped. Add remaining relish ingredients; process until vegetables are finely chopped. Serve with the chicken.

? Did you know?

Lemons change from green to yellow because of cooling nightime temperatures in fall. That's why in tropical areas, lemons with green patches may be perfectly ripe. Just avoid any that have brown patches.

CHICKEN FLORENTINE MEATBALLS

Served over squash and a chunky mushroom-tomato sauce, these tender meatballs are top-notch when it comes to flavor.
—**DIANE NEMITZ** LUDINGTON, MI

Chicken Florentine Meatballs

PREP: 40 MIN. • **COOK:** 20 MIN.
MAKES: 6 SERVINGS

- 2 **eggs, lightly beaten**
- 1 **package (10 ounces) frozen chopped spinach, thawed and squeezed dry**
- ½ **cup dry bread crumbs**
- ¼ **cup grated Parmesan cheese**
- 1 **tablespoon dried minced onion**
- 1 **garlic clove, minced**
- ¼ **teaspoon salt**
- ⅛ **teaspoon pepper**
- 1 **pound ground chicken**
- 1 **medium spaghetti squash**

SAUCE
- ½ **pound sliced fresh mushrooms**
- 2 **teaspoons olive oil**
- 1 **can (14½ ounces) diced tomatoes, undrained**
- 1 **can (8 ounces) tomato sauce**
- 2 **tablespoons minced fresh parsley**
- 1 **garlic clove, minced**
- 1 **teaspoon dried oregano**
- 1 **teaspoon dried basil**

1. In a large bowl, combine the first eight ingredients. Crumble chicken over mixture and mix well. Shape into 1½-in. balls.

2. Place meatballs on a rack in a shallow baking pan. Bake, uncovered, at 400° for 20-25 minutes or until no longer pink. Meanwhile, cut squash in half lengthwise; discard seeds. Place squash cut side down on a microwave-safe plate. Microwave, uncovered, on high for 15-18 minutes or until tender.

3. For sauce, in a large nonstick skillet, saute mushrooms in oil until tender. Stir in the remaining ingredients. Bring to a boil. Reduce heat; simmer, uncovered, for 8-10 minutes or until slightly thickened. Add meatballs and heat through.

4. When squash is cool enough to handle, use a fork to separate strands. Serve with meatballs and sauce.

NOTE *This recipe was tested in a 1,100-watt microwave.*

Savory Rubbed Roast Chicken

A blend of paprika, onion powder, garlic and cayenne go on the skin and inside the cavity to create a delicious, slightly spicy roast chicken. The aroma of this dish while it's cooking drives my family nuts.
—**MARGARET COLE** IMPERIAL, MO

PREP: 20 MIN.
BAKE: 2 HOURS + STANDING
MAKES: 8 SERVINGS

- 2 **teaspoons paprika**
- 1 **teaspoon salt**
- 1 **teaspoon onion powder**
- 1 **teaspoon dried thyme**
- 1 **teaspoon white pepper**
- 1 **teaspoon cayenne pepper**
- ¾ **teaspoon garlic powder**
- ½ **teaspoon pepper**
- 1 **roasting chicken (6 to 7 pounds)**
- 1 **large onion, peeled and quartered**

1. In a small bowl, combine the seasonings; set aside. Place chicken breast side up on a rack in a shallow roasting pan; pat dry. Tuck wings under chicken; tie drumsticks together. Rub seasoning mixture over the outside and inside of chicken. Place onion inside cavity.

2. Bake, uncovered, at 350° for 2 to 2½ hours or until a thermometer inserted in the thigh reads 180°, basting occasionally with pan drippings. (Cover loosely with foil if chicken browns too quickly.) Cover and let stand for 15 minutes before carving.

Chicken in Every Potpie

I created a new title for my mom's potpie recipe while trying to come up with a clever menu for our Presidents' Day Party. An old political slogan came to mind that fit the theme and my main dish just fine.
—**MARY BETH DE RIBEAUX**
GAITHERSBURG, MD

PREP: 20 MIN. • **BAKE:** 30 MIN.
MAKES: 8 SERVINGS

- 4 **cups cubed cooked chicken**
- 1½ **cups chicken broth**
- 1½ **cups frozen peas**
- 3 **to 4 medium carrots, cut into ¼-inch slices**
- 1 **can (10¾ ounces) condensed cream of mushroom soup, undiluted**
- ¼ **teaspoon salt**
- ¼ **teaspoon pepper**
- 2 **cups biscuit/baking mix**
- 1¼ **cups milk**
- 1 **teaspoon garlic powder**
- ½ **teaspoon celery seed**
  Paprika

1. In a large saucepan, combine the chicken, broth, peas, carrots, soup, salt and pepper; bring to a boil, stirring occasionally.

2. Meanwhile, combine the biscuit mix, milk, garlic powder and celery seed (mixture will be thin).

3. Pour hot chicken mixture into eight greased ovenproof 10-oz. custard cups or casseroles. Immediately spoon ¼ cup of biscuit mixture evenly on top of each. Sprinkle with paprika.

4. Bake, uncovered, at 350° for 30-35 minutes or until topping is golden brown.

CHICKEN IN EVERY POTPIE

Indian Baked Chicken

Cumin and turmeric give this hearty entree just the right amount of Indian flavor while maintaining mass appeal for any picky eaters in the bunch.

—**STEPHANIE KURIN** MUNCIE, IN

PREP: 15 MIN. • **BAKE:** 1 HOUR

MAKES: 6 SERVINGS

- 1 **pound small red potatoes, quartered**
- 4 **medium carrots, cut into 1-inch pieces**
- 1 **large onion, cut into 1-inch pieces**
- 6 **boneless skinless chicken thighs (about 1½ pounds)**
- 1 **can (14½ ounces) chicken broth**
- 1 **can (6 ounces) tomato paste**
- 2 **tablespoons olive oil**
- 1 **tablespoon ground turmeric**
- 1 **teaspoon chili powder**
- 1 **teaspoon ground cumin**
- ½ **teaspoon salt**
- ½ **teaspoon garlic powder**
- ½ **teaspoon pepper**

1. Place the potatoes, carrots and onion in a greased 13-in. x 9-in. baking dish; add chicken. In a small bowl, combine the remaining ingredients and pour over top.

2. Cover and bake at 400° for 1 to 1¼ hours or until a meat thermometer inserted into chicken reads 180° and vegetables are tender.

INDIAN BAKED CHICKEN

CHICKEN POTPIE WITH
CHEDDAR BISCUIT TOPPING

Chicken Potpie with Cheddar Biscuit Topping

With chunks of chicken, veggies and a golden biscuit topping, this makes a hearty meal that will rival homey dishes from Mom.

—**SALA HOUTZER** GOLDSBORO, NC

PREP: 20 MIN. • **BAKE:** 45 MIN. • **MAKES:** 9 SERVINGS

- 4 **cups cubed cooked chicken**
- 1 **package (12 ounces) frozen broccoli and cheese sauce**
- 1 **can (10¾ ounces) condensed cream of chicken and mushroom soup, undiluted**
- 1 **can (10¾ ounces) condensed cream of chicken soup, undiluted**
- 2 **medium potatoes, cubed**
- ¾ **cup chicken broth**
- ⅔ **cup sour cream**
- ½ **cup frozen peas**
- ¼ **teaspoon pepper**

TOPPING

- 1½ **cups biscuit/baking mix**
- ¾ **cup shredded sharp cheddar cheese**
- ¾ **cup 2% milk**
- 3 **tablespoons butter, melted**

1. In Dutch oven, combine the first nine ingredients; bring to a boil. Transfer to a greased 13-in. x 9-in. baking dish.

2. In a small bowl, combine the topping ingredients; spoon over top. Bake, uncovered, at 350° for 40-45 minutes or until bubbly and topping is golden brown. Let stand for 10 minutes before serving.

Parmesan Baked Chicken

This no-fuss recipe has been a longtime hit with my family. After a few minutes of prep, the oven does the rest of the work.

—**JANET FALDOWSKI-MCFARLAN** GAHANNA, OH

PREP: 10 MIN. • **BAKE:** 30 MIN.
MAKES: 6 SERVINGS

- 1 **cup biscuit/baking mix**
- ¼ **cup grated Parmesan cheese**
- 1 **teaspoon paprika**
- ½ **teaspoon salt**
- ½ **teaspoon pepper**
- ⅛ **teaspoon garlic powder**
- 1 **broiler/fryer chicken (3 to 4 pounds), cut up**
- ¼ **cup butter, melted**

1. In a large resealable plastic bag, combine the baking mix, cheese, paprika, salt, pepper and garlic powder. Add chicken, a few pieces at a time, and shake to coat.
2. Drizzle butter into a 15-in. x 10-in. x 1-in. baking pan. Place chicken, skin side down, in pan.
3. Bake, uncovered, at 425° for 20 minutes. Turn chicken over; bake 10-15 minutes longer or until juices run clear.

PARMESAN
BAKED CHICKEN

CHICKEN 'N' BISCUITS

Chicken 'n' Biscuits

My chicken with biscuits is a home-style meal that has a colorful medley of vegetables and chunky chicken. The golden homemade biscuits on top make it a top choice when the weather turns cool.

—**MARILYN MINNICK** HILLSBORO, IN

PREP: 25 MIN. • **BAKE:** 30 MIN. • **MAKES:** 8 SERVINGS

- 1 **medium onion, chopped**
- 2 **teaspoons canola oil**
- ¼ **cup all-purpose flour**
- ½ **teaspoon dried basil**
- ½ **teaspoon dried thyme**
- ¼ **teaspoon pepper**
- 2½ **cups fat-free milk**
- 1 **tablespoon Worcestershire sauce**
- 1 **package (16 ounces) frozen mixed vegetables**
- 2 **cups cubed cooked chicken**
- 2 **tablespoons grated Parmesan cheese**

BISCUITS
- 1 **cup all-purpose flour**
- 1 **tablespoon sugar**
- 1½ **teaspoons baking powder**
- ¼ **teaspoon salt**
- ⅓ **cup fat-free milk**
- 3 **tablespoons canola oil**
- 1 **tablespoon minced fresh parsley**

1. In a large saucepan, saute onion in oil until tender. Stir in the flour, basil, thyme and pepper until blended. Gradually stir in milk and Worcestershire sauce until smooth. Bring to a boil; cook and stir for 2 minutes or until thickened. Stir in the vegetables, chicken and cheese; reduce heat to low.
2. Meanwhile, in a large bowl, combine the flour, sugar, baking powder and salt. In a small bowl, combine the milk, oil and parsley; stir into dry ingredients just until combined.
3. Transfer hot chicken mixture to a greased 2½-qt. baking dish. Drop biscuit batter by rounded tablespoonfuls onto chicken mixture.
4. Bake, uncovered, at 375° for 30-40 minutes or until biscuits are lightly browned.

Phyllo Chicken Potpie

Ribbons of buttery phyllo dough provide a crispy topping for this impressive entree. Pearl onions, mushrooms, asparagus and chicken are treated to a creamy sauce flavored with thyme and sherry.

—TASTE OF HOME TEST KITCHEN

PREP: 35 MIN. • **BAKE:** 10 MIN.
MAKES: 6 SERVINGS

- 6 cups water
- 2 cups fresh pearl onions
- 1½ pounds boneless skinless chicken breasts, cubed
- 2 tablespoons canola oil, divided
- 2 medium red potatoes, peeled and chopped
- 1 cup sliced fresh mushrooms
- 1 can (14½ ounces) reduced-sodium chicken broth
- ½ pound fresh asparagus, trimmed and cut into 1-inch pieces
- 3 tablespoons sherry or additional reduced-sodium chicken broth
- 3 tablespoons cornstarch
- ½ cup fat-free milk
- 1½ teaspoons minced fresh thyme
- ½ teaspoon salt
- ¼ teaspoon pepper
- 10 sheets phyllo dough (14 inches x 9 inches)
  Refrigerated butter-flavored spray

1. In a Dutch oven, bring water to a boil. Add pearl onions; boil for 3 minutes. Drain and rinse in cold water; peel and set aside.

2. In a large skillet, cook chicken in 1 tablespoon oil over medium heat until no longer pink; remove and keep warm. In the same pan, saute potatoes in remaining oil for 5 minutes. Add onions and mushrooms; saute 3 minutes longer. Add the broth, asparagus and sherry or additional broth. Bring to a boil. Reduce heat; cover and simmer for 5 minutes or until potatoes are tender.

3. Combine cornstarch and milk until smooth; stir into skillet. Bring to a boil; cook and stir for 2 minutes or until thickened. Drain chicken; add to onion mixture. Stir in the thyme, salt and pepper. Transfer to an 8-in. square baking dish coated with cooking spray.

4. Stack all 10 phyllo sheets. Roll up, starting at a long side; cut into ½-in. strips. Place in a large bowl and toss to separate strips. Spritz with butter-flavored spray. Arrange over chicken mixture; spritz again.

5. Bake, uncovered, at 425° for 10-15 minutes or until golden brown.

Chicken and Dumpling Casserole

Basil adds the right touch of flavor and makes the whole house smell good while this dish cooks. My husband loves the fluffy dumplings with plenty of gravy poured over them.

—SUE MACKEY JACKSON, WI

PREP: 30 MIN. • **BAKE:** 40 MIN.
MAKES: 6-8 SERVINGS

- ½ cup chopped onion
- ½ cup chopped celery
- ¼ cup butter, cubed
- 2 garlic cloves, minced
- ½ cup all-purpose flour
- 2 teaspoons sugar
- 1 teaspoon salt
- 1 teaspoon dried basil
- ½ teaspoon pepper
- 4 cups chicken broth
- 1 package (10 ounces) frozen green peas
- 4 cups cubed cooked chicken

DUMPLINGS
- 2 cups biscuit/baking mix
- 2 teaspoons dried basil
- ⅔ cup 2% milk

1. In a large saucepan, saute onion and celery in butter until tender. Add garlic; cook 1 minute longer. Stir in the flour, sugar, salt, basil and pepper until blended. Gradually add broth; bring to a boil. Cook and stir for 1 minute or until thickened; reduce heat. Add peas and cook for 5 minutes, stirring constantly. Stir in chicken. Pour into a greased 13-in. x 9-in. baking dish.

2. For dumplings, in a small bowl, combine baking mix and basil. Stir in milk with a fork until moistened. Drop by tablespoonfuls into 12 mounds over chicken mixture.

3. Bake, uncovered, at 350° for 30 minutes. Cover and bake 10 minutes longer or until a toothpick inserted in a dumpling comes out clean.

PHYLLO CHICKEN POTPIE

EASY CHICKEN
AND DRESSING

Easy Chicken and Dressing

I've always enjoyed trying new recipes, and now that our children are grown, I have more time to do just that! But recipes like this are worth keeping for a comforting chicken dinner.

—**ANNE SMITH** TAYLORS, SC

PREP: 15 MIN. + STANDING • **BAKE:** 55 MIN.
MAKES: 8 SERVINGS

- 1 cup chopped onion
- 1 cup chopped celery
- ¼ cup butter, cubed
- 2 cups chicken broth
- 1½ teaspoons dried thyme
- 1 teaspoon poultry seasoning
- ½ teaspoon salt
- ½ teaspoon pepper
- ¼ teaspoon ground nutmeg
- 2 eggs, lightly beaten or ½ cup egg substitute
- 1 package (12 ounces) unseasoned stuffing cubes
- ¼ cup minced fresh parsley
- 3 cups cubed cooked chicken
- 1 can (10¾ ounces) condensed cream of chicken or mushroom soup, undiluted
- ⅓ cup water

1. In a large saucepan, saute onion and celery in butter until tender; remove from the heat. Stir in the broth, seasonings and eggs. Add bread cubes and parsley; toss to coat.
2. Transfer to a greased 13-in. x 9-in. baking dish. Top with chicken. Combine soup and water; spoon over chicken. Let stand for 10 minutes.
3. Cover and bake at 350° for 50 minutes. Uncover; bake 5-10 minutes longer or until a thermometer reads 160°.

Chicken Meat Loaf with Mushroom Gravy

Try a twist on traditional meat loaf with this delightful chicken version. Here, ketchup is replaced with an easy mushroom and wine sauce for a more upscale topping.

—**KERI SCHOFIELD LAWSON** BREA, CA

PREP: 25 MIN. • **BAKE:** 55 MIN. + STANDING
MAKES: 10 SERVINGS

- 1¼ pounds boneless skinless chicken breast halves
- 1¼ pounds boneless skinless chicken thighs
- 2 eggs, lightly beaten
- ½ cup panko (Japanese) bread crumbs
- ½ cup mayonnaise
- 1 envelope onion soup mix
- 2 tablespoons minced fresh parsley
- 1 tablespoon prepared horseradish
- ½ teaspoon salt
- ½ teaspoon garlic powder
- ½ teaspoon dried sage leaves
- ½ teaspoon dried thyme
- ½ teaspoon pepper

GRAVY
- 2 cups sliced fresh mushrooms
- 1 tablespoon butter
- 3 cups reduced-sodium chicken broth
- 1 teaspoon dried rosemary, crushed
- ½ teaspoon salt
- ¼ teaspoon white pepper
- 3 tablespoons cornstarch
- ¼ cup white wine or additional reduced-sodium chicken broth

1. Place chicken in the freezer for 15-20 minutes or until it begins to freeze. Cut into 1-in. pieces. In a food processor, cover and process chicken in batches until ground.
2. In a large bowl, combine the eggs, bread crumbs, mayonnaise, soup mix, parsley, horseradish, salt, garlic powder, sage, thyme and pepper. Crumble chicken over mixture and mix well.
3. Shape into a loaf; place in a greased 13-in. x 9-in. baking dish. Bake, uncovered, at 350° for 55-60 minutes or until no pink remains and a meat thermometer reads 165°. Let stand for 10 minutes.
4. Meanwhile, in a large saucepan, saute mushrooms in butter until tender. Add the broth, rosemary, salt and white pepper. Bring to a boil. Combine cornstarch and wine until smooth; gradually stir into mushroom mixture. Bring to a boil; cook and stir for 2 minutes or until thickened.
5. Slice chicken loaf; serve with gravy.
NOTE *You may substitute 2½ pounds ground chicken for the chicken breast halves and thighs.*

almonds. Serve immediately. Pour the remaining mixture into a greased 13-in. x 9-in. baking dish; cool. Sprinkle with remaining almonds. Cover and freeze for up to 3 months.

To use frozen casserole *Thaw in the refrigerator overnight. Cover and bake at 350° for 40-45 minutes or until heated through.*

So-Easy Chicken Tagine

Aromatic, warm and sweet, the spices in this simple chicken tagine dish will warm your belly. It's an easy way to prepare chicken thighs, which often are less expensive than chicken breast halves.

—**VERONICA GANTLEY** NORFOLK, VA

PREP: 20 MIN. • **BAKE:** 45 MIN.
MAKES: 6 SERVINGS

- 2 **pounds boneless skinless chicken thighs, cut into 2-inch pieces**
- 2 **medium sweet potatoes, peeled and cut into 2-inch pieces**
- 1 **cup chicken broth**
- 1 **small onion, coarsely chopped**
- 2 **tablespoons honey**
- 1 **tablespoon olive oil**
- 1 **teaspoon pepper**
- 1 **teaspoon ground allspice**
- ¼ **teaspoon salt**
  Dash ground cinnamon
  Dash ground nutmeg
- 1 **cup dried cranberries**
- ¾ **cup chopped pistachios, toasted**
  Hot cooked couscous, optional

1. In a Dutch oven, combine the first 11 ingredients. Cover and bake at 400° for 30 minutes.

2. Uncover; sprinkle with cranberries. Bake 15-20 minutes longer or until chicken is no longer pink. Sprinkle with pistachios. Serve with couscous if desired.

Wild Rice Chicken Dinner

With chicken, green beans and the crunch of water chestnuts and almonds, this casserole has everything you need. Using ready-to-serve wild rice makes putting it together a breeze.

—**LORRAINE HANSON** INDEPENDENCE, IA

START TO FINISH: 30 MIN.
MAKES: 2 CASSEROLES
(6-8 SERVINGS EACH)

- 2 **packages (8.8 ounces each) ready-to-serve long grain and wild rice**
- 2 **packages (16 ounces each) frozen French-style green beans, thawed**
- 2 **cans (10¾ ounces each) condensed cream of celery soup, undiluted**
- 2 **cans (8 ounces each) sliced water chestnuts, drained**
- ⅔ **cup chopped onion**
- 2 **jars (4 ounces each) sliced pimientos, drained**
- 1 **cup mayonnaise**
- ½ **cup 2% milk**
- 1 **teaspoon pepper**
- 6 **cups cubed cooked chicken**
- 1 **cup slivered almonds, divided**

1. Heat rice according to package directions. Meanwhile, in a Dutch oven, combine the green beans, soup, water chestnuts, onion, pimientos, mayonnaise, milk and pepper. Bring to a boil. Reduce heat; cover and simmer for 5 minutes. Stir in chicken and rice; cook 3-4 minutes longer or until chicken is heated through.

2. Transfer half of the mixture to a serving dish; sprinkle with ½ cup

WILD RICE
CHICKEN DINNER

Quick Math

When cooking a whole chicken with the intent of using the meat in various recipes, remember: A 3 1/2-pound whole chicken will yield about 3 cups of diced cooked chicken.

top tip

Bacon-Cheese Topped Chicken

Mushrooms, bacon strips and Monterey Jack cheese top these tender marinated chicken breasts that provide a flavorful dining experience. I get compliments whenever I serve them. They're among my family's favorites.

—**MELANIE KENNEDY** BATTLE GROUND, WA

PREP: 40 MIN. + MARINATING
BAKE: 20 MIN. • **MAKES:** 4 SERVINGS

- ½ cup Dijon mustard
- ½ cup honey
- 4½ teaspoons canola oil, divided
- ½ teaspoon lemon juice
- 4 boneless skinless chicken breast halves
- ¼ teaspoon salt
- ⅛ teaspoon pepper
  Dash paprika
- 2 cups sliced fresh mushrooms
- 2 tablespoons butter
- 1 cup (4 ounces) shredded Monterey Jack cheese
- 1 cup (4 ounces) shredded cheddar cheese
- 8 bacon strips, partially cooked
- 2 teaspoons minced fresh parsley

BACON-CHEESE TOPPED CHICKEN

1. In a small bowl, combine the mustard, honey, 1½ teaspoons oil and lemon juice. Pour ½ cup into a large resealable plastic bag; add the chicken. Seal the bag and turn to coat; refrigerate for 2 hours. Cover and refrigerate the remaining marinade.
2. Drain and discard marinade from chicken. In a large skillet over medium heat, brown chicken in remaining oil on all sides. Sprinkle with salt, pepper and paprika. Transfer to a greased 11-in. x 7-in. baking dish.
3. In the same skillet, saute mushrooms in butter until tender. Spoon reserved marinade over chicken. Top with cheeses and mushrooms. Place bacon strips in a crisscross pattern over chicken.
4. Bake, uncovered, at 375° for 20-25 minutes or until a meat thermometer reads 170°. Sprinkle with parsley.

Creamy Almond Chicken

The buttery almond coating gives this dish a rich flavor that stands out from ordinary breaded chicken.

—**DIANA FRANKFORT** SARASOTA, FL

PREP: 15 MIN. • **BAKE:** 1 HOUR
MAKES: 4 SERVINGS

- ¾ cup all-purpose flour
- 1 broiler/fryer chicken (3 to 3½ pounds), cut up
- 8 tablespoons butter, melted, divided
- 1 teaspoon each salt, paprika and celery salt
- ¾ cup sliced almonds
- 1½ cups half-and-half cream
- 1 cup (8 ounces) sour cream
- 3 tablespoons dry bread crumbs

1. Place flour in a large resealable plastic bag; add chicken, a few pieces at a time. Seal bag; shake to coat. In a shallow dish, combine 7 tablespoons butter, salt, paprika and celery salt. Add chicken pieces and turn to coat.
2. Transfer to a greased 13-in. x 9-in. baking dish. Sprinkle with almonds. Pour cream around chicken. Cover and bake at 350° for 45 minutes. Drain, reserving ½ cup sauce.
3. Stir sour cream into sauce; pour over the chicken. Combine bread crumbs with the remaining butter; sprinkle over chicken. Bake, uncovered, 15 minutes more or until chicken juices run clear.

White Lasagna

Next time you have leftover chicken or turkey, try this lasagna. I like to serve it with a simple salad and hot garlic bread.

—**GAYLE BECKER** MT. CLEMENS, MI

PREP: 25 MIN. • **BAKE:** 35 MIN.
MAKES: 8-10 SERVINGS

- 9 lasagna noodles
- ¼ cup butter, cubed
- ⅓ cup all-purpose flour
- 1 tablespoon minced dried onion
- ¼ teaspoon garlic powder
- ⅛ teaspoon pepper
- 2 cups chicken or turkey broth
- 1 cup milk
- 1 cup grated Parmesan or Romano cheese, divided
- 1 can (4 ounces) sliced mushrooms, drained
- 1 package (10 ounces) frozen cut asparagus or ¾ pound fresh cut asparagus, cooked and drained
- 2 cups cubed cooked chicken or turkey
- 1 package (6 ounces) sliced or shredded mozzarella cheese
- 6 ounces thinly sliced cooked ham, chopped

1. Cook noodles according to package directions. Drain.
2. In a large saucepan, melt butter; blend in flour, onion, garlic powder and pepper. Add broth and milk; cook and stir until bubbly and thickened. Stir in ½ cup Parmesan cheese.
3. Spread ½ cup sauce in the bottom of a greased 13-in. x 9-in. baking pan. Stir mushrooms into the remaining sauce. Lay 3 noodles in the pan. Top with asparagus, chicken, mozzarella and about 1 cup sauce. Top with 3 more noodles, the cooked ham and half of the remaining sauce. Cover with remaining noodles and sauce. Sprinkle with the remaining Parmesan cheese.
4. Bake, uncovered, at 350° for 35 minutes or until heated through.

CAJUN CHICKEN
PASTA BAKE

Cajun Chicken Pasta Bake

My family loves pasta, so I decided to get in the kitchen and come up with my own chicken pasta. This recipe is quick and simple to make, and it tastes so good, they all go back for seconds.

—KIM WEISHUHN PENSACOLA, FL

PREP: 30 MIN. • **BAKE:** 20 MIN.
MAKES: 2 CASSEROLES (6 SERVINGS EACH)

- 2 packages (12 ounces each) bow tie pasta
- 2 pounds boneless skinless chicken breasts, cut into 1-inch strips
- 2 tablespoons olive oil, divided
- 2 bunches green onions, chopped
- 2 medium green peppers, chopped
- 2 medium sweet red peppers, chopped
- 1 can (14½ ounces) reduced-sodium chicken broth
- 2 cans (10¾ ounces each) condensed cream of chicken soup, undiluted
- 1 can (10¾ ounces) condensed cream of mushroom soup, undiluted
- ¾ cup 2% milk
- 2½ teaspoons Cajun seasoning
- 1½ teaspoons garlic powder
- 2 cups (8 ounces) shredded Colby-Monterey Jack cheese

1. Cook pasta according to package directions to al dente.
2. Meanwhile, in a Dutch oven, saute chicken in 1 tablespoon oil until juices run clear. Remove with a slotted spoon and set aside. In the same pan, saute onions and peppers in remaining oil until tender. Add the broth, soups, milk, Cajun seasoning and garlic powder. Bring to a boil and remove from the heat.
3. Drain pasta. Add pasta and chicken to soup mixture; toss to coat. Divide between two greased 13-in. x 9-in. baking dishes. Sprinkle with cheese. Cover and bake casseroles at 350° for 20-25 minutes or until bubbly.
Freeze option *Cool unbaked casseroles; cover and freeze. To use, partially thaw in refrigerator overnight. Remove from refrigerator 30 minutes before baking. Preheat oven to 350°. Bake casseroles, as directed, increasing time as necessary to heat through, until a thermometer inserted in center reaches 165°.*

Broccoli Chicken Stuffed Shells

These cheesy stuffed shells can be assembled ahead of time and popped in the oven just before dinner. I like to round out the meal with a tossed salad and warm bread.

—KAREN JAGGER COLUMBIA CITY, IN

PREP: 15 MIN. • **BAKE:** 30 MIN.
MAKES: 7 SERVINGS

- 1 jar (16 ounces) Alfredo sauce
- 2 cups frozen chopped broccoli, thawed
- 2 cups diced cooked chicken
- 1 cup (4 ounces) shredded cheddar cheese
- ¼ cup shredded Parmesan cheese
- 21 jumbo pasta shells, cooked and drained

1. In a large bowl, combine the Alfredo sauce, broccoli, chicken and cheeses. Spoon into pasta shells. Place in a greased 13-in. x 9-in. baking dish.
2. Cover and bake at 350° for 30-35 minutes or until heated through.

Chicken Breast with Stuffing

Meals for one don't have to be boring or fussy. This flavorful chicken and stuffing entree bakes in a foil packet in the oven for easy clean up.

—BOBBY TAYLOR LAPORTE, IN

PREP: 10 MIN. • **BAKE:** 45 MIN.
MAKES: 1 SERVING.

- 1 bone-in chicken breast half (7 ounces)
- ¼ teaspoon salt
- ⅛ teaspoon pepper
- 1 tablespoon chopped onion
- 1 tablespoon chopped celery
- 1 tablespoon butter
- ¼ teaspoon minced fresh parsley
- ⅛ teaspoon dried thyme
- ⅛ teaspoon dried basil
- 1 drop hot pepper sauce
- 1 slice day-old bread, cubed

1. Place chicken skin side down on a double thickness of heavy-duty foil lightly coated with cooking spray; sprinkle with salt and pepper.
2. In a skillet, saute onion and celery in butter until tender. Stir in the remaining ingredients. Spoon over chicken. Fold foil around chicken and seal tightly; place in a baking pan. Bake at 400° for 40-45 minutes. Carefully open foil. Bake 5 minutes longer or until chicken juices run clear.

BROCCOLI CHICKEN STUFFED SHELLS

**ZESTY
CHICKEN MARINARA**
PAGE 95

Slow Cooker

SLOW-COOKED
CHICKEN CHILI

Slow-Cooked Chicken Chili

Lime juice gives this chili a zesty twist, while canned tomatoes and beans make preparation a breeze. It's fun to serve with toasted tortilla strips.

—DIANE RANDAZZO SINKING SPRING, PA

PREP: 25 MIN. • **COOK:** 40 MIN.
MAKES: 6 SERVING

- 1 medium onion, chopped
- 1 each medium sweet yellow, red and green pepper, chopped
- 2 Tbsp. olive oil
- 3 garlic cloves, minced
- 1 lb. ground chicken
- 2 cans (14½ oz. each) diced tomatoes, undrained
- 1 can (15 oz.) white kidney or cannellini beans, rinsed and drained
- ¼ cup lime juice
- 1 Tbsp. all-purpose flour
- 1 Tbsp. baking cocoa
- 1 Tbsp. ground cumin
- 1 Tbsp. chili powder
- 2 tsp. ground coriander
- 1 tsp. grated lime peel
- ½ tsp. salt
- ½ tsp. garlic pepper blend
- ¼ tsp. pepper
- 2 flour tortillas (8 in.), cut into ¼-in. strips
- 6 Tbsp. reduced-fat sour cream

1. In a large skillet, saute onion and peppers in oil for 7-8 minutes or until crisp-tender. Add garlic; cook 1 minute longer. Add chicken; cook and stir over medium heat for 8-9 minutes or until meat is no longer pink.
2. Transfer to a 3-qt. slow cooker. Stir in the tomatoes, beans, lime juice, flour, cocoa, cumin, chili powder, coriander, lime peel, salt, garlic pepper and pepper.
3. Cover and cook on low for 4-5 hours or until heated through.
4. Place tortilla strips on a baking sheet coated with cooking spray. Bake at 400° for 8-10 minutes or until crisp. Serve chili with sour cream and tortilla strips.

Hearty Chicken Noodle Soup

This satisfying homemade soup with a hint of cayenne is brimming with vegetables, chicken and noodles. The recipe came from my father-in-law, but I made some adjustments to give it my own spin.

—NORMA REYNOLDS OVERLAND PARK, KS

PREP: 20 MIN. • **COOK:** 5½ HOURS
MAKES: 12 SERVINGS (3 QUARTS)

- 12 fresh baby carrots, cut into ½-inch pieces
- 4 celery ribs, cut into ½-inch pieces
- ¾ cup finely chopped onion
- 1 tablespoon minced fresh parsley
- ½ teaspoon pepper
- ¼ teaspoon cayenne pepper
- 1½ teaspoons mustard seed
- 2 garlic cloves, peeled and halved
- 1¼ pounds boneless skinless chicken breast halves
- 1¼ pounds boneless skinless chicken thighs
- 4 cans (14½ ounces each) chicken broth
- 1 package (9 ounces) refrigerated linguine

1. In a 5-qt. slow cooker, combine the first six ingredients. Place mustard seed and garlic on a double thickness of cheesecloth; bring up corners of cloth and tie with kitchen string to form a bag. Place in slow cooker. Add chicken and broth. Cover and cook on low for 5-6 hours or until meat is tender.
2. Discard spice bag. Remove chicken; cool slightly. Stir linguine into soup; cover and cook on high for 30 minutes or until tender. Cut chicken into pieces and return to soup; heat through.

HEARTY CHICKEN NOODLE SOUP

Sweet Pepper Chicken

Sweet red and green pepper strips add attractive color to this delicious chicken. Put it in the slow-cooker before getting ready for church on Sunday morning. It'll be ready to eat by the time you get home.

—**ANN JOHNSON** DUNN, NC

PREP: 10 MIN. • **COOK:** 4 HOURS • **MAKES:** 6 SERVINGS

- 6 bone-in chicken breast halves (8 ounces each), skin removed
- 1 tablespoon canola oil
- 2 cups sliced fresh mushrooms
- 1 medium onion, halved and sliced
- 1 medium green pepper, julienned
- 1 medium sweet red pepper, julienned
- 1 can (10¾ ounces) condensed cream of chicken soup, undiluted
- 1 can (10¾ ounces) condensed cream of mushroom soup, undiluted
   Hot cooked rice

1. In a large skillet, brown chicken in oil on both sides. Transfer to a 5-qt. slow cooker. Top with mushrooms, onion and peppers. Combine the soups; pour over vegetables.
2. Cover and cook on low for 4-5 hours or until a thermometer reads 170°. Serve with rice.

Citrus Chicken

For a nutritious meal, I serve this chicken with broccoli and rice. It's a recipe that dates back to 1976 when I got my first slow-cooker, which is still in use today.

—**BARBARA EASTON** NORTH VANCOUVER, BC

PREP: 15 MIN. • **COOK:** 4 HOURS • **MAKES:** 4 SERVINGS

- 2 medium oranges, cut into wedges
- 1 medium green pepper, chopped
- 1 broiler/fryer chicken (3 to 4 pounds), cut up and skin removed
- 1 cup orange juice
- ½ cup chili sauce
- 2 tablespoons soy sauce
- 1 tablespoon molasses
- 1 teaspoon ground mustard
- 1 teaspoon minced garlic
- ¼ teaspoon pepper
   Hot cooked rice

Place oranges and green pepper in a 5-qt. slow cooker coated with cooking spray. Top with chicken. Combine the next seven ingredients; pour over chicken. Cover and cook on low for 4-5 hours or until chicken juices run clear. Serve with rice.

SWEET PEPPER CHICKEN

Party-Time Wings

Here are some irresistible, fall-off-the-bone chicken wings. Chili sauce and powder give them just a bit of heat, while molasses lends a hint of sweetness. They also make a great meal with rice.

—**SHARON MORCILIO** JOSHUA TREE, CA

PREP: 15 MIN. • **COOK:** 8 HOURS • **MAKES:** ABOUT 4 DOZEN

- 5 pounds chicken wings (about 25 wings)
- 1 bottle (12 ounces) chili sauce
- ¼ cup lemon juice
- ¼ cup molasses
- 2 tablespoons Worcestershire sauce
- 6 garlic cloves, minced
- 1 tablespoon chili powder
- 1 tablespoon salsa
- 1 teaspoon garlic salt
- 3 drops hot pepper sauce

1. Cut chicken wings into three sections; discard wing tips. Place the wings in a 5-qt. slow cooker.

2. In a small bowl, combine the remaining ingredients; pour over chicken. Stir to coat. Cover and cook on low for 6-8 hours or until chicken is tender.

NOTE *Uncooked chicken wing sections (wingettes) may be substituted for whole chicken wings.*

COCONUT CURRY CHICKEN

Coconut Curry Chicken

My husband and I love this yummy dish! It's a breeze to prepare in the slow cooker, and it tastes just like a meal you'd have at your favorite Indian or Thai restaurant.

—**ANDI KAUFFMAN** BEAVERCREEK, OR

PREP: 20 MIN. • **COOK:** 5 HOURS • **MAKES:** 4 SERVINGS

- 2 medium potatoes, peeled and cubed
- 1 small onion, chopped
- 4 boneless skinless chicken breast halves (4 ounces each)
- 1 cup light coconut milk
- 4 teaspoons curry powder
- 1 garlic clove, minced
- 1 teaspoon reduced-sodium chicken bouillon granules
- ¼ teaspoon salt
- ¼ teaspoon pepper
- 2 cups hot cooked rice
- ¼ cup thinly sliced green onions
  Raisins, flaked coconut and chopped unsalted peanuts, optional

1. Place potatoes and onion in a 3- or 4-qt. slow cooker. In a large nonstick skillet coated with cooking spray, brown chicken on both sides.

2. Transfer to slow cooker. In a small bowl, combine the coconut milk, curry, garlic, bouillon, salt and pepper; pour over chicken. Cover and cook on low for 5-6 hours or until meat is tender.

3. Serve chicken and sauce with rice; sprinkle with green onions. Garnish with raisins, coconut and peanuts if desired.

PARTY-TIME WINGS

Spring-Thyme Chicken Stew

During a long winter (and spring), when my husband and I are in need of something warm, comforting and bright, we make this stew. It reminds me of the days my mom would make chicken soup.

—**AMY CHASE** VANDERHOOF, BC

PREP: 15 MIN. • **COOK:** 7 HOURS
MAKES: 4 SERVINGS

- 1 **pound small red potatoes, halved**
- 1 **large onion, finely chopped**
- ¾ **cup shredded carrots**
- 3 **tablespoons all-purpose flour**
- 6 **garlic cloves, minced**
- 2 **teaspoons grated lemon peel**
- 2 **teaspoons dried thyme**
- ½ **teaspoon salt**
- ¼ **teaspoon pepper**
- 1½ **pounds boneless skinless chicken thighs, halved**
- 2 **cups reduced-sodium chicken broth**
- 2 **bay leaves**
- 2 **tablespoons minced fresh parsley**

1. Place potatoes, onion and carrots in a 3-qt. slow cooker. Sprinkle with flour, garlic, lemon peel, thyme, salt and pepper; toss to coat. Place chicken over top. Add broth and bay leaves.
2. Cook, covered, on low 7-9 hours or until chicken and vegetables are tender. Remove bay leaves. Sprinkle with parsley.

SPRING-THYME CHICKEN STEW

HOT WING DIP

Hot Wing Dip

Since I usually have all the ingredients on hand, this is a great go-to snack for entertaining friends and family.

—**COLEEN CORNER** GROVE CITY, PA

PREP: 10 MIN. • **COOK:** 1 HOUR
MAKES: 4½ CUPS

- 2 **cups shredded cooked chicken**
- 1 **package (8 ounces) cream cheese, cubed**
- 2 **cups (8 ounces) shredded cheddar cheese**
- 1 **cup ranch salad dressing**
- ½ **cup Louisiana-style hot sauce**
  Tortilla chips and/or celery sticks
  Minced fresh parsley, optional

In a 3-qt. slow cooker, combine the chicken, cream cheese, cheddar cheese, salad dressing and hot sauce. Cover and cook on low for 1-2 hours or until cheese is melted. Serve with chips and/or celery. Sprinkle with parsley if desired.

Chicken Athena

With olives, sun-dried tomatoes, lemon juice and garlic, this easy chicken dish is full of classic Greek flavors. Serve it with orzo or couscous for a tasty accompaniment.

—**RADELLE KNAPPENBERGER** OVIEDO, FL

PREP: 15 MIN. • **COOK:** 4 HOURS
MAKES: 6 SERVINGS

- 6 **boneless skinless chicken breast halves (6 ounces each)**
- 2 **medium onions, chopped**
- ⅓ **cup sun-dried tomatoes (not packed in oil), chopped**
- ⅓ **cup pitted Greek olives, chopped**
- 2 **tablespoons lemon juice**
- 1 **tablespoon balsamic vinegar**
- 3 **garlic cloves, minced**
- ½ **teaspoon salt**

Place chicken in a 3-qt. slow cooker. Add the remaining ingredients. Cover and cook on low for 4 hours or until a thermometer reads 170°.

Zesty Chicken Marinara

A friend served this delicious Italian-style chicken before a church social, and I fell in love with it. My husband says it tastes like something you'd get at a restaurant.
—**LINDA BAUMANN** RICHFIELD, WI

PREP: 15 MIN. • **COOK:** 4 HOURS
MAKES: 4 SERVINGS

- 4 bone-in chicken breast halves (12 to 14 ounces each), skin removed
- 2 cups marinara sauce
- 1 medium tomato, chopped
- ½ cup Italian salad dressing
- 1½ teaspoons Italian seasoning
- 1 garlic clove, minced
- ½ pound uncooked angel hair pasta
- ½ cup shredded part-skim mozzarella cheese

1. Place chicken in a 4-qt. slow cooker. In a small bowl, combine the marinara sauce, tomato, salad dressing, Italian seasoning and garlic; pour over chicken. Cover and cook on low for 4-5 hours or until chicken is tender.
2. Cook pasta according to package directions; drain. Serve chicken and sauce with pasta; sprinkle with cheese.

ZESTY CHICKEN MARINARA

Slow-Cooker BBQ Chicken

Of all the recipes I make in my slow-cooker, this is my favorite. The BBQ is sweet with a little bit of spice.
—**YVONNE MCKIM** VANCOUVER, WA

PREP: 15 MIN. • **COOK:** 5 HOURS
MAKES: 12 SERVINGS

- 6 chicken leg quarters, skin removed
- ¾ cup ketchup
- ½ cup orange juice
- ¼ cup packed brown sugar
- ¼ cup red wine vinegar
- ¼ cup olive oil
- 4 teaspoons minced fresh parsley
- 2 teaspoons Worcestershire sauce
- 1 teaspoon garlic salt
- ½ teaspoon pepper
- 2 tablespoons plus 2 teaspoons cornstarch
- ¼ cup water

1. With a sharp knife, cut leg quarters at the joints. Place chicken in a 4-qt. slow cooker.
2. In a small bowl, combine the ketchup, orange juice, brown sugar, vinegar, oil, parsley, Worcestershire sauce, garlic salt and pepper; pour over chicken. Cover and cook on low for 5-6 hours or until meat is tender.
3. Remove chicken to a serving platter; keep warm. Skim fat from cooking juices; transfer 2 cups to a small saucepan. Bring liquid to a boil.
4. Combine cornstarch and water until smooth. Gradually stir into pan. Bring to boil; cook and stir for 2 minutes or until thickened. Serve with chicken.

Chili-Lime Chicken Tostadas

The flavor of this tender chicken is delicious with a hint of lime. It has just the right amount of heat.
—**LAURA POWELL** SOUTH JORDAN, UT

PREP: 10 MIN. • **COOK:** 5 HOURS
MAKES: 5 SERVINGS

- 4 pounds bone-in chicken breast halves, skin removed
- 1 medium onion, chopped
- 1 can (4 ounces) chopped green chilies

CHILI-LIME CHICKEN TOSTADAS

- 3 tablespoons lime juice
- 4½ teaspoons chili powder
- 4 garlic cloves, minced
- 10 tostada shells
- 1 can (16 ounces) fat-free refried beans
    Optional ingredients: Shredded cabbage, shredded cheddar cheese, salsa, sour cream, sliced ripe olives and guacamole

1. In a 4-qt. slow cooker, combine chicken and onion. In a small bowl, combine the green chilies, lime juice, chili powder and garlic; pour over chicken. Cover and cook on low for 5-6 hours or until meat is tender.
2. Remove chicken; cool slightly. Set aside ⅔ cup cooking juices. Discard remaining juices. Shred chicken with two forks and return to slow cooker. Stir in reserved cooking juices.
3. Spread tostadas with refried beans; top with chicken. Layer with cabbage, cheese, salsa, sour cream, olives and guacamole if desired.

Did you know?

Milk, cream and sour cream break down during extended cooking, so it's important to add dairy only during the last 15-30 minutes of cooking. Stir it in until heated through but do not simmer or boil.

Teriyaki Chicken Thighs

The teriyaki flavor really comes through in this lip-smacking chicken dinner, and the meat practically falls off the bone. I serve it with hot rice to soak up the extra sauce.

—GIGI MILLER STOUGHTON, WI

PREP: 15 MIN. • **COOK:** 4 HOURS
MAKES: 6 SERVINGS

- 12 **boneless skinless chicken thighs (about 3 pounds)**
- ¾ **cup sugar**
- ¾ **cup soy sauce**
- 6 **tablespoons cider vinegar**
- ¾ **teaspoon ground ginger**
- ¾ **teaspoon minced garlic**
- ¼ **teaspoon pepper**
- 4½ **teaspoons cornstarch**
- 4½ **teaspoons cold water**
  Hot cooked rice, optional

1. Place chicken in a 4-qt. slow cooker. Combine the sugar, soy sauce, vinegar, ginger, garlic and pepper; pour over chicken. Cover and cook on low for 4-5 hours or until chicken is tender.
2. Remove chicken to a serving platter; keep warm. Skim fat from cooking juices; transfer to a small saucepan. Bring liquid to a boil. Combine cornstarch and water until smooth. Gradually stir into the pan. Bring to a boil; cook and stir for 2 minutes or until thickened. Serve with chicken and rice if desired.

TERIYAKI CHICKEN THIGHS

Peachy Chicken with Sweet Potatoes

When my mother was pregnant with me, one of the only things she could eat was home-canned peaches. To this day, I love recipes with peaches.

—SANDRA BONOW LEWISTON, MN

PREP: 25 MIN. • **COOK:** 6 HOURS
MAKES: 4 SERVINGS

- 2 **medium sweet potatoes, peeled and cubed**
- 1 **medium onion, chopped**
- 8 **boneless skinless chicken thighs (about 2 pounds)**
- 1 **teaspoon paprika**
- 1 **teaspoon dried thyme**
- ½ **teaspoon salt**
- ⅛ **teaspoon cayenne pepper**
- 1 **cup peach preserves**
- 2 **tablespoons cornstarch**
- ½ **cup cold water**

1. In a 4- or 5-qt. slow cooker, combine sweet potatoes and onion. Sprinkle chicken with paprika, thyme, salt and cayenne; arrange over sweet potatoes. Top with preserves. Cover and cook on low for 6-8 hours or until chicken and potatoes are tender.
2. Remove chicken and vegetables to a serving platter; keep warm. Skim fat from cooking juices; transfer to a small saucepan. Bring liquid to a boil. Combine cornstarch and water until smooth. Gradually stir into the pan. Bring to a boil; cook and stir for 2 minutes or until thickened. Serve with chicken and vegetables.

top tip No Peeking

Every time you lift the top of a slow cooker, steam is lost and you will have to add about 15 minutes on to the cooking time. So unless a recipe instructs you to add ingredients during cooking, keep a lid on it.

These baked potatoes are meals in themselves, with a smoky barbecue flavor that will make your mouth water. You can top them with your favorite cheese and garnish. —**AMBER MASSEY** ARGYLE, TX

BBQ Chicken Baked Potatoes

PREP: 15 MIN. • **COOK:** 6 HOURS
MAKES: 10 SERVINGS

- 4½ **pounds bone-in chicken breast halves, skin removed**
- 2 **tablespoons garlic powder**
- 1 **large red onion, sliced into thick rings**
- 1 **bottle (18 ounces) honey barbecue sauce**
- 1 **cup Italian salad dressing**
- ½ **cup packed brown sugar**
- ½ **cup cider vinegar**
- ¼ **cup Worcestershire sauce**
- 2 **tablespoons liquid smoke, optional**
- 10 **medium potatoes, baked**
  Crumbled blue cheese and chopped green onions, optional

1. Place chicken in a greased 5- or 6-qt. slow cooker; sprinkle with garlic powder and top with onion. Combine the barbecue sauce, salad dressing, brown sugar, vinegar, Worcestershire sauce and liquid smoke if desired; pour over chicken.

2. Cover and cook on low for 6-8 hours or until chicken is tender. When cool enough to handle, remove the chicken from bones; discard bones and onion. Skim fat from cooking juices.

3. Shred meat with two forks and return to slow cooker; heat through. Serve with potatoes, blue cheese and green onions if desired.

**CHICKEN AND
MUSHROOM CREPES**
PAGE 100

Let's Celebrate!

{ **BEST-EVER
FRIED CHICKEN**
PAGE 101 }

{ **RICE-STUFFED
GAME HENS**
PAGE 102 }

{ **BUFFALO
CHICKEN LASAGNA**
PAGE 106 }

Chicken & Mushroom Crepes

This makes a lovely anniversary dinner. I've been married to a "meat and potatoes" man for more than 40 years, and was happy to hear him rave about this dish.

—**JOANNE SIEG** RIVER HILLS, MB

PREP: 30 MIN. • **COOK:** 15 MIN. • **MAKES:** 5 SERVINGS

- ¼ cup butter, cubed
- ½ pound sliced fresh mushrooms
- ¼ cup finely chopped onion
- ¼ cup all-purpose flour
- 2 cups 2% milk
- 2 teaspoons chicken bouillon granules
- ½ teaspoon Italian seasoning
- ¼ teaspoon pepper
- ½ cup sour cream
- 3 tablespoons sherry or chicken broth
- 2 cups finely chopped cooked chicken
- 2 tablespoons minced fresh parsley, divided
- 15 prepared crepes (9 inches)
  Additional sour cream, optional

1. In a large skillet over medium-high heat, melt butter. Add mushrooms and onion; saute until tender. Sprinkle with flour; stir until blended. Gradually add milk. Stir in the bouillon, Italian seasoning and pepper.

2. Bring to a boil; cook and stir for 2 minutes or until thickened. Stir in sour cream and sherry. Remove 1 cup sauce; set aside. Stir chicken and 1 tablespoon parsley into remaining mixture; heat through.

3. Spread 3 tablespoons filling down the center of each crepe; roll up. Drizzle reserved sauce over the top. Sprinkle with remaining parsley. Serve with additional sour cream if desired.

CHICKEN AND
MUSHROOM CREPES

Thai Chicken Lettuce Wraps

This springtime lunch is a treat to share at the end of the school year. The teachers and staff have fun putting them together.

—**LAUREEN PITTMAN** RIVERSIDE, CA

PREP: 35 MIN. • **MAKES:** 6 SERVINGS

- ¼ cup rice vinegar
- 2 tablespoons lime juice
- 2 tablespoons reduced-fat mayonnaise
- 2 tablespoons reduced-fat creamy peanut butter
- 1 tablespoon brown sugar
- 1 tablespoon reduced-sodium soy sauce
- 2 teaspoons minced fresh gingerroot
- 1 teaspoon sesame oil
- 1 teaspoon Thai chili sauce
- 1 garlic clove, chopped
- 3 tablespoons canola oil
- ½ cup minced fresh cilantro

CHICKEN SALAD

- 2 cups cubed cooked chicken breast
- 1 small sweet red pepper, diced
- ½ cup chopped green onions
- ½ cup shredded carrot
- ½ cup unsalted dry roasted peanuts, chopped, divided
- 6 Bibb or Boston lettuce leaves

1. In a blender, combine the first 10 ingredients. While processing, gradually add oil in a steady stream; stir in cilantro. Set aside.

2. In a large bowl, combine the chicken, red pepper, onions, carrot and ¼ cup peanuts. Add dressing and toss to coat. Divide among lettuce leaves; sprinkle with remaining peanuts. Fold lettuce over filling.

Best-Ever Fried Chicken

Crispy, juicy and perfectly seasoned, this fried chicken lives up to its name. Summer reunions and neighborhood gatherings will never be the same.
—**LOLA CLIFTON** VINTON, VA

PREP: 15 MIN. • **COOK:** 15 MIN. • **MAKES:** 4 SERVINGS

- 2 cups all-purpose flour
- 1 tablespoon dried thyme
- 1 tablespoon paprika
- 2 teaspoons salt
- 1 teaspoon pepper
- ⅓ cup milk
- 1 egg
- 2 tablespoons lemon juice
- 1 broiler/fryer chicken (3 to 4 pounds), cut up
  Oil for deep-fat frying

1. In a shallow bowl, mix the first five ingredients. In a separate shallow bowl, whisk the milk, egg and lemon juice. Coat chicken pieces, one at a time, with flour mixture; dip in milk mixture, then coat again with flour mixture.
2. In an electric skillet or deep-fat fryer, heat oil to 375°. Fry chicken, a few pieces at a time, for 6-10 minutes on each side or until chicken juices run clear. Drain on paper towels.

MARGARITA CHICKEN

BEST-EVER FRIED CHICKEN

Margarita Chicken

Marinated in flavors of garlic and lime, this tangy grilled chicken is ready to go whenever the coals are hot! Serve with roasted corn on the cob and lemonade for summer eating at its most relaxed.
—**KELLY BRUNEMAN** CEDAR PARK, TX

PREP: 10 MIN. + MARINATING • **GRILL:** 10 MIN. • **MAKES:** 4 SERVINGS

- 1 can (10 ounces) frozen non-alcoholic margarita mix, thawed
- 3 tablespoons lime juice
- 3 garlic cloves, minced
- 4 boneless skinless chicken breast halves (6 ounces each)
- ¼ teaspoon salt
- ¼ teaspoon pepper

1. In a small bowl, combine the margarita mix, lime juice and garlic. Pour 1 cup marinade into a large resealable plastic bag. Add the chicken; seal bag and turn to coat. Refrigerate for 2-4 hours. Cover and refrigerate remaining marinade.
2. Drain and discard marinade. Sprinkle chicken with salt and pepper. Using long-handled tongs, moisten a paper towel with cooking oil and lightly coat the grill rack.
3. Grill chicken, covered, over medium heat or broil 4 in. from the heat for 5-7 minutes on each side or until a meat thermometer reads 160°, basting frequently with reserved marinade.

Chicken Marsala Lasagna

I love Chicken Marsala, but most recipes do not serve a crowd. This is a version I developed to serve a dozen, and it's perfect as a winter potluck.
—**DEBBIE SHANNON** RINGGOLD, GA

PREP: 50 MIN. • **BAKE:** 55 MIN. + STANDING
MAKES: 12 SERVINGS

- 4 teaspoons Italian seasoning, divided
- 1 teaspoon salt
- ¾ pound boneless skinless chicken breasts, cubed
- 1 tablespoon olive oil
- ¼ cup finely chopped onion
- ½ cup butter, cubed
- 12 garlic cloves, minced
- ½ pound sliced baby portobello mushrooms
- 1½ cups beef broth
- ¾ cup marsala wine, divided
- ¼ teaspoon coarsely ground pepper
- 3 tablespoons cornstarch
- ½ cup finely chopped fully cooked ham
- 1 carton (15 ounces) ricotta cheese
- 1 package (10 ounces) frozen chopped spinach, thawed and squeezed dry
- 2 cups (8 ounces) shredded Italian cheese blend
- 1 cup grated Parmesan cheese, divided
- 2 eggs, lightly beaten
- 12 lasagna noodles, cooked, rinsed and drained

1. Combine 2 teaspoons Italian seasoning and salt; sprinkle over chicken. In a large skillet, saute chicken in oil until no longer pink. Remove and keep warm.
2. In the same skillet, cook onion in butter over medium heat for 2 minutes. Add garlic; cook 2 minutes longer. Stir in mushrooms; cook 4-5 minutes longer or until tender.
3. Stir in the broth, ½ cup wine and pepper; bring to a boil. Combine the cornstarch and remaining wine until smooth; stir into the pan. Bring to a boil; cook and stir for 2 minutes or until thickened. Stir in ham and chicken.
4. In a large bowl, combine the ricotta cheese, spinach, Italian cheese blend, ¾ cup Parmesan cheese, eggs and remaining Italian seasoning. Spread 1 cup chicken mixture into a greased 13-in. x 9-in. baking dish. Layer with three noodles, about ¾ cup chicken mixture and about 1 cup ricotta mixture. Repeat layers three times.
5. Cover and bake at 350° for 40 minutes. Sprinkle with remaining Parmesan cheese. Bake, uncovered, for 10-15 minutes or until bubbly and cheese is melted. Let stand for 10 minutes before cutting.

RICE-STUFFED GAME HENS

Rice-Stuffed Game Hens

I first served these hens at Thanksgiving one year when only a few of us gathered to celebrate the holiday. They're so yummy they often grace our table throughout the year.
—**JENNY HOLLIDAY** ROANOKE, AL

PREP: 20 MIN. • **BAKE:** 65 MIN.
MAKES: 4 SERVINGS

- 1 package (6.2 ounces) fast-cooking long grain and wild rice mix
- 2 celery ribs, chopped
- 1 small onion, chopped
- 2 tablespoons butter, divided
- 1 can (10¾ ounces) condensed cream of mushroom soup, undiluted
- 1 can (4 ounces) mushroom stems and pieces, drained
- 4 Cornish game hens (20 to 24 ounces each)
- ¼ teaspoon salt
- ¼ teaspoon pepper

6. Cook rice according to package directions. In a small skillet, saute celery and onion in 1 tablespoon butter until tender. Stir in the soup, mushrooms and prepared rice.
7. Sprinkle inside and outside of hens with salt and pepper. Stuff with rice mixture. Place on a rack in a greased shallow roasting pan; cover with foil.
8. Bake at 350° for 40 minutes. Remove foil. Melt remaining butter; brush over hens. Bake 25-35 minutes longer or until juices run clear and a meat thermometer reads 180° for hens and 165° for stuffing.

CHICKEN MARSALA LASAGNA

Flattening a chicken breast can be somewhat theraputic after a long day. Use this easy method to relieve some stress while putting a winning dinner on the table.

1 Hold a sharp knife parallel to cutting board along one long side of breast; cut almost in half, leaving breast attached at one side.

2 Open breast so it lies flat; cover with plastic wrap. Using flat side of a meat mallet, lightly pound to 1/4-in. thickness.

3 Remove plastic wrap and stuff according to recipe. Some recipes say to place filling in the center, while others instruct you to place filling on one side.

4 Roll up jelly roll-style, tucking in sides. Or, if placing the filling on one half, fold the chicken over the stuffing. Secure with toothpicks.

Chicken Stuffed with Walnuts, Apples & Brie

I came up with this recipe one afternoon at work when all I could think about is what I was going to fix for dinner. It turned out even better than I expected and makes a nice alternative to ham or turkey during the holidays.

—NICOLE PAVELICH LEXINGTON, KY

PREP: 20 MIN. • **COOK:** 25 MIN.
MAKES: 2 SERVINGS

- ¼ **cup chopped onion**
- 3 **tablespoons butter, divided**
- ½ **cup chopped peeled apple**
- 2 **tablespoons chopped walnuts, toasted**
- ⅛ **teaspoon dried rosemary, crushed**
  Dash plus ¼ teaspoon salt, divided
  Dash plus ¼ teaspoon pepper, divided
- 2 **boneless skinless chicken breast halves (6 ounces each)**
- ⅛ **teaspoon garlic powder**
- 2 **ounces Brie cheese, cubed**
- ¼ **cup cider vinegar**
- ¾ **cup unsweetened apple juice, divided**
- 1½ **teaspoons cornstarch**

1. In a large skillet, saute onion in 1 tablespoon butter for 1 minute. Add apple; cook 2-3 minutes longer or until apple is golden brown. Remove from the heat; add walnuts, rosemary, and a dash of salt and pepper.
2. Flatten chicken to ¼-in. thickness; sprinkle with garlic powder and remaining salt and pepper. Place apple mixture and Brie on half of each chicken breast; fold chicken over. Secure with toothpicks if necessary.
3. In the same skillet, brown chicken in remaining butter. Stir in vinegar and ¼ cup apple juice. Bring to a boil. Reduce heat; cover and cook for 15-20 minutes or until a thermometer reads 170°.
4. Remove chicken to a serving platter; discard toothpicks. Combine cornstarch and remaining apple juice; add to the pan. Bring to a boil; cook and stir for 2 minutes or until thickened. Serve with chicken.

SMOKY GARLIC AND
SPICE CHICKEN

Fall grilling calls for some
smoking recipes. This one
gets its rich flavor from
an overnight lime and soy
sauce-marinade.

—TINA REPAK MIRILOVICH JOHNSTOWN, PA

Smoky Garlic and Spice Chicken

PREP: 20 MIN. + MARINATING • **GRILL:** 1 HR +
STANDING

MAKES: 4 SERVINGS

- ⅓ cup reduced-sodium soy sauce
- 3 tablespoons lime juice
- 6 garlic cloves, minced
- 1 tablespoon olive oil
- 1 tablespoon ground cumin
- 1 teaspoon paprika
- ½ teaspoon dried oregano
- ½ teaspoon pepper
- 1 broiler/fryer chicken (3 to 4 pounds), split in half lengthwise

1. In a large resealable plastic bag, combine the first eight ingredients. Add the chicken; seal bag and turn to coat. Refrigerate for 8 hours or overnight.

2. Drain and discard marinade. Moisten a paper towel with cooking oil; using long-handled tongs, lightly coat the grill rack. Prepare grill for indirect heat, using a drip pan.

3. Place chicken cut side down over drip pan and grill, covered, over indirect medium heat for 1 to 1¼ hours or until a meat thermometer reads 180°, turning occasionally. Let stand for 10 minutes before carving.

top tip Halving a Chicken

Place the chicken breast side down with neck end pointing away from you. Using a large knife or kitchen shears, cut out and remove the backbone. Then cut through the breastbone in a firm motion. Finally, rearrange the skin to cover the chicken breast during cooking.

Fig & Wine-Sauced Chicken Kabobs

The combination of grilled chicken and mushrooms in a sweet fig sauce can only be described as exquisite.

—**BARBARA WHEELER** ROYAL OAK, MI

PREP: 1 HOUR + MARINATING
GRILL: 15 MIN. • **MAKES:** 6 SERVINGS

- 5 **small onions, divided**
- ½ **cup olive oil**
- 2 **garlic cloves, minced**
- 1½ **pounds boneless skinless chicken breasts, cut into 1-inch cubes**
- 1¼ **pounds dried figs**
- 2½ **cups sweet white wine**
- 3 **tablespoons orange marmalade**
- 2 **tablespoons fig preserves**
- 2 **tablespoons lemon juice**
- ½ **teaspoon salt**
- ¼ **teaspoon white pepper**
- ½ **pound small fresh portobello mushrooms**
  Hot cooked rice
  Fresh mint leaves and lemon wedges, optional

1. Grate two onions; place in a large resealable plastic bag. Add the oil, garlic and chicken; seal bag and turn to coat. Refrigerate for 8 hours or overnight.

2. Meanwhile, in a large saucepan, bring figs and wine to a boil. Reduce heat; simmer, uncovered, for 50-60 minutes or until figs are plumped and tender. Remove figs; keep warm. Bring liquid to a boil; cook until reduced to ⅔ cup. Add the marmalade, preserves, lemon juice, salt and pepper. Cook and stir for 5-6 minutes or until slightly thickened.

3. Cut remaining onions into 1-in. pieces. Drain chicken; discard marinade. On six metal or soaked wooden skewers, alternately thread the chicken, onions and mushrooms.

4. Using long-handled tongs, moisten a paper towel with cooking oil and lightly coat the grill rack. Grill kabobs, covered, over medium heat or broil 4 in. from the heat for 10-15 minutes or until juices run clear, turning occasionally.

5. Serve kabobs with rice and reserved figs; drizzle with sauce. Garnish with mint and lemon if desired.

Crab-Stuffed Chicken Breasts

Who knew you could prepare a dinner like this using the microwave? Served over hot pasta, you can have a restaurant-style entree on the table in just 30 minutes.

—**PAT DURRIE** OMAHA, NE

START TO FINISH: 30 MIN.
MAKES: 4 SERVINGS

- 4 **boneless skinless chicken breast halves**
- ½ **cup lump crabmeat, drained**
- ½ **cup dry bread crumbs**
- ¼ **cup grated Parmesan cheese**
- 1 **teaspoon garlic powder**
- 1 **teaspoon onion powder**
- 1 **teaspoon dried basil**
- 2 **cups meatless spaghetti sauce**
- ½ **cup shredded part-skim mozzarella cheese**
  Hot cooked pasta, optional

1. Flatten chicken to ¼-in. thickness; top with crab. Roll up tightly and secure with toothpicks. In a shallow bowl, combine the bread crumbs, Parmesan cheese, garlic powder, onion powder and basil. Roll chicken in crumb mixture; set remaining mixture aside.

2. Place chicken in a shallow 1½-qt. microwave-safe dish coated with cooking spray. Cover and microwave on high for 2-3 minutes. Turn the chicken; sprinkle with reserved crumb mixture. Cover and cook for 2-3 minutes longer or until chicken juices run clear.

3. Top with spaghetti sauce. Cover and microwave on high for 2-3 minutes or until heated through. Sprinkle with cheese; heat, uncovered, for 30-60 seconds or until the cheese is melted. Let stand for 5 minutes. Serve over pasta if desired.

NOTE *This recipe was tested in a 1,100-watt microwave.*

FIG AND WINE-SAUCED CHICKEN KABOBS

BUFFALO CHICKEN LASAGNA

Buffalo Chicken Lasagna

This recipe was inspired by my daughter's favorite food—buffalo wings! It tastes just like it came from a restaurant, and it's perfect for game day potlucks.

—**MELISSA MILLWOOD** LYMAN, SC

PREP: 1 HOUR 40 MIN.
BAKE: 40 MIN. + STANDING
MAKES: 12 SERVINGS

- 1 tablespoon canola oil
- 1½ pounds ground chicken
- 1 small onion, chopped
- 1 celery rib, finely chopped
- 1 large carrot, grated
- 2 garlic cloves, minced
- 1 can (14½ ounces) diced tomatoes, drained
- 1 bottle (12 ounces) buffalo wing sauce
- ½ cup water
- 1½ teaspoons Italian seasoning
- ½ teaspoon salt
- ¼ teaspoon pepper
- 9 lasagna noodles
- 1 carton (15 ounces) ricotta cheese
- 1¾ cups (7 ounces) crumbled blue cheese, divided
- ½ cup minced Italian flat leaf parsley
- 1 egg, lightly beaten
- 3 cups (12 ounces) shredded part-skim mozzarella cheese
- 2 cups (8 ounces) shredded white cheddar cheese

1. In a Dutch oven, heat oil over medium heat. Add the chicken, onion, celery and carrot; cook and stir until meat is no longer pink and vegetables are tender. Add garlic; cook 2 minutes longer. Stir in the tomatoes, wing sauce, water, Italian seasoning, salt and pepper; bring to a boil. Reduce heat; cover and simmer for 1 hour.

2. Meanwhile, cook noodles according to package directions; drain. In a small bowl, mix the ricotta cheese, ¾ cup blue cheese, parsley and egg.

3. Spread 1½ cups sauce into a greased 13-in. x 9-in. baking dish. Layer with three noodles, 1½ cups sauce, ⅔ cup ricotta mixture, 1 cup mozzarella cheese, ⅔ cup cheddar cheese and ⅓ cup blue cheese. Repeat layers twice.

4. Bake, covered, at 350° for 20 minutes. Uncover; bake 20-25 minutes longer or until bubbly and cheese is melted. Let stand for 10 minutes before serving.

SERVES ②

Orange-Glazed Cornish Hens

When I make these succulent stuffed Cornish hens, my husband's only complaint is that he gets full before he's ready to quit eating!

—**CATHY BROKER** MERIDIAN, ID

PREP: 35 MIN. • **BAKE:** 70 MIN.
MAKES: 2 SERVINGS

- 3 bacon strips, diced
- ½ cup finely shredded carrot
- ¼ cup chopped onion
- 1½ cups unseasoned stuffing cubes
- 2 tablespoons minced fresh parsley
- ¼ teaspoon dried savory
  Dash pepper
- ¾ teaspoon chicken bouillon granules, divided
- 2 tablespoons hot water
- 2 Cornish game hens (20 to 24 ounces each)
- 1 tablespoon canola oil
- ¼ cup white wine or apple juice
- 2 tablespoons plus ⅔ cup orange juice, divided
- 1 tablespoon butter
- 1 tablespoon brown sugar
- 1½ teaspoons cornstarch

1. In a small skillet, cook bacon over medium heat until crisp. Remove with a slotted spoon to paper towels. In the drippings, saute carrot and onion until tender; transfer to a large bowl. Stir in stuffing cubes, parsley, savory, pepper and bacon.

2. Dissolve ¼ teaspoon bouillon in hot water; pour over stuffing mixture and gently toss to moisten. Spoon into hens. Tuck wings under hens; tie legs together.

3. Place on a greased rack in a roasting pan. Lightly brush hens with oil; loosely cover with foil. Bake at 375° for 30 minutes.

4. Meanwhile, in a saucepan, bring the wine, 2 tablespoons orange juice and butter to a boil. Remove from the heat; set aside ¼ cup for sauce and keep warm.

5. Brush remaining mixture over hens. Bake 40-50 minutes longer or until meat juices run clear and a thermometer inserted in stuffing reads 165°, brushing every 15 minutes with glaze.

6. For sauce, in a small saucepan, combine the brown sugar, cornstarch, and remaining bouillon and orange juice until smooth. Stir in reserved glaze. Bring to a boil; cook and stir for 1-2 minutes or until thickened. Serve with hens.

ORANGE-GLAZED CORNISH HENS

Stuffing a chicken or turkey adds additional flavors and aromatics to the meat. Try different combinations of herbs and citrus zest to suit your family's tastes.

❶ Tuck wings under chicken. Loosely stuff chicken with stuffing, allowing about 3/4 cup per pound of poultry. To ensure even cooking, do not overstuff the bird.

❷ Place breast side up on a rack in a large roasting pan. Tie the drumsticks together and season according to the recipe.

Christmas Chicken Cordon Bleu

Christmas Eve wouldn't be complete without my dad's Chicken Cordon Bleu! My husband tries all year to talk Dad into making this scrumptious main dish for other occasions. It's a definite family favorite.

—VICKIE LEMOS MODESTO, CA

PREP: 10 MIN. • **COOK:** 50 MIN.
MAKES: 6 SERVINGS

- 6 **boneless skinless chicken breast halves (4 ounces each)**
- 3 **thin slices fully cooked ham, halved**
- 3 **slices Swiss cheese, halved**
- ½ **cup all-purpose flour**
- ½ **teaspoon salt**
- ¼ **teaspoon paprika**
- 1 **egg**
- 2 **tablespoons milk**
- ¾ **cup dry bread crumbs**
- 3 **tablespoons butter**
- 1 **cup chicken broth**
- 2 **tablespoons dried parsley flakes**
  Hot cooked rice

- 1 **can (10¾ ounces) condensed cream of chicken soup, undiluted**
- ½ **cup sour cream**

1. Flatten chicken breast to ¼-in. thickness; layer each with one piece of ham and one piece of cheese. Roll up each jelly-roll style, starting with a short side; secure with toothpicks.
2. In a shallow bowl, combine the flour, salt and paprika. In another bowl, beat egg and milk. Place bread crumbs in a third bowl. Dredge chicken in flour mixture, dip in egg mixture, then roll in bread crumbs.
3. In a skillet over medium heat, brown chicken in butter. Add the broth and parsley. Cover and simmer over medium-low heat for 40-50 minutes or until a meat thermometer reads 170°.
4. Remove toothpicks. Place rice on a serving platter; top with chicken and keep warm. Combine soup and sour cream; heat through but do not boil. Serve with chicken and rice.

Roast Chicken with Oyster Stuffing

The aroma of this roasted chicken is almost as wonderful as its flavor, and the oyster stuffing is to die for. If you're not crazy about turkey dinners, try this instead for a lovely holiday meal.

—JOANN JENSEN LOWELL, IN

PREP: 35 MIN. • **BAKE:** 2 HOURS + STANDING
MAKES: 6 SERVINGS (4 CUPS STUFFING)

- 1 **can (8 ounces) whole oysters**
- 1 **celery rib, chopped**
- 1 **small onion, chopped**
- ¼ **cup butter, cubed**
- 2 **tablespoons minced fresh parsley**
- ½ **teaspoon Italian seasoning**
- 3 **cups cubed bread, lightly toasted**
- 1 **roasting chicken (6 to 7 pounds)**
- ¼ **cup butter, melted**
- 1 **to 2 teaspoons paprika**

1. Drain oysters, reserving liquid; coarsely chop oysters. Set aside. In a small skillet, saute celery and onion in butter until tender. Stir in parsley and Italian seasoning. Place bread cubes in a large bowl; add the butter mixture, oysters and ¼ cup reserved oyster liquid.
2. Just before baking, loosely stuff chicken with stuffing. Place breast side up on a rack in a large roasting pan; tie drumsticks together. Combine melted butter and paprika; spoon over chicken.
3. Bake, uncovered, at 350° for 2 to 2½ hours or until a thermometer reads 180° for chicken and 165° for stuffing, basting occasionally with pan drippings. (Cover loosely with foil if chicken browns too quickly.)
4. Cover chicken and let stand for 10 minutes before removing stuffing and carving. Skim fat and thicken pan juices if desired.

❓ Did you know?

In Japan, a customary Christmas Day dinner includes a bucket of Kentucky Fried Chicken. Crowds of people line up outside every branch in the country, while other Japanese families pre-order their bucket months in advance.

GENERAL INDEX

This index lists every recipe by food category, cooking method and/or major ingredient, so you can easily locate the recipes that best suit your tastes.

ALPHABETICAL INDEX

This index lists all of the recipes in this book by title, making it easy to find your family's favorite dishes.

INDEXES